why niebuhr matters

Yale UNIVERSITY PRESS

new haven and

london

charles

lemert

why

niebuhr

matters

Yale University Press books may be purchased in quantity for educational, business, or promotional use. For information, please e-mail sales.press@yale.edu (U.S. office) or sales@yaleup.co.uk (U.K. office).

Set in Adobe Garamond type by IDS Infotech Ltd., Chandigarh, India.
Printed in the United States of America.

Library of Congress Cataloging-in-Publication Data

Lemert, Charles C., 1937–
Why Niebuhr matters / Charles Lemert.
    p.   cm.
Includes bibliographical references (p.   ) and index.
ISBN 978-0-300-17542-4 (cloth : alk. paper) 1. Niebuhr, Reinhold, 1892–1971. I. Title.
BX4827.N5L46 2011
230′.044092—dc22   2011014580

A catalogue record for this book is available from the British Library.

This paper meets the requirements of ANSI/NISO z39.48–1992 (Permanence of Paper).

10 9 8 7 6 5 4 3 2 1

Also by Charles Lemert

The Structural Lie: Small Clues to Global Things

*Uncertain Worlds: World-Systems Analysis in
    Changing Times*, with Immanuel Wallerstein and
    Carlos Aguirre Rojas

Globalization: The Basics

Ethics in a New Millennium, with Sam Han

Globalization: A Reader, with Anthony Elliott,
    Daniel Chaffee, and Eric Hsu

The Race of Time: A Charles Lemert Reader, edited
    by Daniel Chaffee and Sam Han

The New Individualism, with Anthony Elliott

*Thinking the Unthinkable: The Riddles of Classical
    Social Theories*

Durkheim's Ghosts: Cultural Logics and Social Things

Deadly Worlds: The Emotional Costs of Globalization,
    with Anthony Elliott

The Souls of W. E. B. Du Bois, with Alford A. Young,
    Jr., Jerry G. Watts, Manning Marable, and
    Elizabeth Higginbotham

Social Things

Postmodernism Is Not What You Think

Sociology After the Crisis

*Social Theory: The Multicultural and Classical
    Readings*

Muhammad Ali: Trickster and the Culture of Irony

Dark Thoughts: Race and the Eclipse of Society

The Goffman Reader, edited, with introductions, with Ann Branaman

Crime and Deviance: Essays and Innovations by Edwin Lemert, edited, with Michael Winter

The Voice of Anna Julia Cooper, edited, with Esme Bhan

Intellectuals and Politics: Social Theory Beyond the Academy

Michel Foucault: Social Theory and Transgression, with Garth Gillan

French Sociology: Rupture and Renewal Since 1968

Sociology and the Twilight of Man: Homocentrism and Discourse in Sociological Theory

In memory of
Joseph C. Williamson (1933–2008)

contents

Why Niebuhr? xi

one   Reinhold Niebuhr: Tamed Cynic 1

two   Evangelical Preacher: Wheat and Tares 23

three   Powers, Pulpits, and Politics: Moral Man and
        Immoral Society 45

four   Sin, Self, and Society: Nature and Destiny of Man 101

five   Nations, Global Politics, and Religion:
        Irony and American History 145

six   Political Recovery and Globalization:
        Knowing the Difference 193

        Notes 213

        Acknowledgments 237

        Index 239

why niebuhr?

Late April, 2007, a prominent political writer for a major American newspaper interviewed a young and relatively unknown political figure. The writer asked the politician whether he had ever read Reinhold Niebuhr. He said he had, whereupon the writer pressed the point: "What do you take away from him?" The politician's answer:

> I take away . . . the compelling idea that there's serious evil in the world, and hardship and pain. And we should be humble and modest in our belief we can eliminate those things. But we shouldn't use that as an excuse for cynicism and inaction. I take away . . . the sense we have to make these efforts knowing they are hard, and not swinging from naïve idealism to bitter realism.

The writer, David Brooks of the *New York Times*, was impressed. "Pretty good," said Brooks, condescendingly.[1] Two years later, the politician would be president of the United States.

Whether the young president governs successfully, much less in a Niebuhrian manner, will not be known for years to come.

Even his political enemies usually will concede that Barack Obama is smart. Yet sheer intelligence does not get at what was at least "pretty good" in his answer to Brooks.

How could it be that even a very smart American presidential candidate would be asked to summarize the ideas of a thinker whose time had come and gone when he, Obama, was but a schoolboy in Jakarta? Even more, how could Obama have had so ready a retort as to the point of Niebuhr's thinking? More still, what, beyond personal temperament, might have caused him to use language more common to genteel religious thinkers like Niebuhr than to hard-bitten politicians?

"Evil"—much less "serious evil"—does not trip lightly from the tongues of personages of Obama's liberal, even leftish, inclinations. Ronald Reagan's "evil empire" and George W. Bush's "axis of evil" famously appealed in code to very different constituents. But Obama spoke openly, as Niebuhr had, to a deeper political philosophy. He called for stiff political work between naïve idealism and bitter realism—an insistence especially barbed in hard times. Late in 2009, in his acceptance speech for the Nobel Peace Prize, Obama addressed a world at war in similar terms. "We make mistakes," he said, "and fall victim to the temptations of pride, and power, and sometimes evil."[2] Once again, pure Niebuhr. Why?

Since the first few years of the twenty-first century there has been a revival of interest in Reinhold Niebuhr.[3] His books and essays are being reissued. His name is dropped by speakers and commentators. His work has become a subject of controversy.[4] Why Niebuhr now? He was not a politician, nor even a political theorist by training, but a Protestant preacher and teacher of an earlier time.

Niebuhr died in 1971. In his day, he was, as he might be in ours, a moral guide to a politics that took seriously the world as it is. At the height of his powers at mid-twentieth century, Niebuhr was one of a select few able and willing to challenge and rethink the nonsocialist Left in American politics. Today, after a full decade of the twenty-first century, socialism as such (as distinct from the catch-all "socialism" of a good bit of conservative blather) is off the political table, like so many of the applied ideologies that came into their short-lived own in Niebuhr's day. What Niebuhr leaves to our time are his theories and practical politics of an honest, true-to-historical-fact realism—a political realism that refuses to abandon high moral principles to short-term practical compromises.

Why Niebuhr now? One reason for the Niebuhr revival is that these are times marked by two unsettling historical threats to a world system that had prevailed for a good half-millennium. One threat is the religious challenge to the modern ideal of political culture. In America until Obama's election, the evangelical Right seemed to have had the upper political hand and still now remains a force defiant of liberal ideals of progress and democratic justice.[5] Defiance of the ideals and practices of the still most powerful modern state is, of course, also a global phenomenon—and not just by Islamic extremists but by new religious movements in Africa and Central and South America as well as in the surprising Confucian revival in China and East Asia. One way or another, since at least the Enlightenment, religion has been the thorn in the side of modern theories of history and human progress—a particularly irritating thorn because religion was both a source of many of modernity's political ideas and an awkward reminder that the secular modern is rooted in the traditions of a not-so-dead past.

The second threat is the anxiety arising from evidence of a deep structural decline of the global dominance of the West. As the new millennium takes shape, the United States, but Europe also, has been politically challenged from the outside as never before—from the terrorisms of vaguely Islamic fringe actors, by the resource-rich nations from the Arctic and Venezuela to Africa and the Middle East, but also by the economic authority and diplomatic independence of East and South Asia.[6]

So far as one can tell in the short run, both threats are seismic shifts in the global order; and both are strangely connected in ways that are not easily explained by techno-troubles and economic crises—the dark underbellies of globalization.[7]

There have been threatening times before. Empires have fallen. Plagues have decimated civilizations. Many times over war has redrawn the map of the world. New technologies changed daily life. New ideas transformed how people thought. These blows, and more, have been absorbed as the centuries passed one into another. Whether the threats that seem so considerable in our days change us or our children's children is for others after us to determine. All we can do, in the midst of it all, is ask the question that must be asked and answered, at best, partially.

What now? The question turns on the established historical fact that when the worlds change, those living in the transitional moments must adjust how they live—their hopes and dreams, as well as their access to the necessities of daily life. Their most practically urgent question is indeed, *What-now?*—which is to say: What are we to do now that much, perhaps all, that we have been taught to assume as the givens of our lives may no longer apply?

For almost every *What-now?* moment in history there has been a thinker or leader able to pick up the thread of what was unraveling to weave a new cloak out of the remnants. When Rome fell, there was Augustine. When Roman Christendom shook, there were Martin Luther and John Calvin. When classical metaphysics lost it grip, there were Kant, Marx, and Hegel. When the Qing dynasty collapsed, there were Sun Yat-sen and Mao. And on it goes—Phillip, then Alexander; the House of David, then Isaiah and the prophets; Mary, then Elizabeth; Batista, then Castro; Leopold and the Belgians, then Lumumba and Mobuto. Not all who came after were good or helpful; but there were successors and for better or worse they gave what answers there were to *What-now?*

Why Niebuhr? How might his political theories from an earlier time help us to understand and respond to a changing present? His answer, in a word, would be a political realism that sacrifices neither ideals to mere pragmatism nor politics to bitterness and greed. Modern politics as they have been practiced by modern states have followed simply stated values— freedom, liberty, rights, among others of the kind. But these, such as they are in practice, are values that tip so toward the morality of the individual as to sink before the harshly amoral power of large structural forces—economic failures, fascistic states, domestic turmoil, environmental collapse, and the like. For nearly a century now, since at least the dawning of the Great War in 1914, the classically modern ideology of the moral individual has suffered blows dealt by the twentieth century's wars, economic failures, and political extremisms. It has survived, to be sure, but in a much weakened condition as global structures continue to outrun both modernity's ideologies and its reluctance to engage what Niebuhr was inclined to call the evil wrought by large structures.

In his day, Niebuhr was widely celebrated for being the one who fixed the terms of a debate we have since lost sight of. In the decades since his death in 1971, realism has come to mean expediency, evil has become a throwaway term, religious enthusiasms have lost somber connection with their originating scriptures, liberal politics has found itself trapped in a cramped corner between rock reality and the hard place left by years of small-minded selfishness. The times call for intellectual seriousness in the face of realities none alive today could have been taught in childhood to imagine.

Reinhold Niebuhr was a figure of such political and intellectual importance that on the occasion of Harvard's 350th anniversary in 1986, then–professor of history Alan Heimert remarked that only two public figures of the century were of an intellectual and public stature sufficient to the occasion. Their mention cut neatly to the point in that both were dead. Niebuhr was one (the other was Walter Lippmann). But Reinhold Niebuhr is less well remembered today in inverse proportion to the charge his ideas might give to the current situation—a charge, that is, and not a shock.

why niebuhr matters

.

I

reinhold

niebuhr

tamed

cynic

Winters, the farmlands are barren. Time moves slowly. The setting sun softens the late afternoon for an instant. Dark falls hard. Months later, winter is forgotten. The land is flush with cattle and corn. Summer's heat throttles the pulse. The sun sinks late through the cruel humidity. The knowable world nods off for a time, exposing its sweaty nether parts to the night.

Into such a place in 1892 Reinhold Niebuhr was born. Wright City, Missouri, was then a small, isolated town on the near American prairies, huddled in the embrace of the Missouri and Mississippi rivers hard on America's first east-west trail. Today the trail is paved over by a national highway. Interstate 70 crosses the Mississippi River to the west at St. Louis. Road and river cut and quarter the country as they did when the road was dirt. At St. Louis, North ebbs into South as West overtakes East. In Niebuhr's time the sections strained. To imagine Huckleberry Finn's float downriver from Hannibal, near St. Louis, deep into the South at Memphis, you must feel the bitter discrepancy that may never fade. America's South, while decidedly not North, is neither East nor West.

Niebuhr's Wright City is just fifty miles to the west beyond St. Louis, a city swallowed in the gathering currents, more a rest stop than a destination. In the nineteenth century, St. Louis, still young, was already a relic of America's European roots. Its stout German culture could not, even then, anchor it against the forces that tug at places like these. In American lore, vast but fixed spaces excite the restless. From the first openings to the West, American culture learned to think of hope and power as the special promises of these open spaces. Ordinary life, however, requires cramped virtues hardened by the realities of small, if boring, settlements. Getting by in close quarters demands endurance over hard time.

When Niebuhr was born, Wright City was far enough beyond St. Louis to have been where pioneers began to sense the dreadful thrill of the West. Even now, when fields far from city lights are bare, you can feel the difference. Winter's northwesterly winds cut to the bone, thirsty for the rivers they had been seeking since they left the Rocky Mountains. In the nineteenth century, the land and the waters produced strong but modest young men and women, willing to husband the land and cultivate the nation.

They were the stock that came from afar to claim the land and a new life. To them Reinhold Niebuhr was born. From them, he learned that America had to outgrow the innocence it was reluctant to shed.

Gustav Niebuhr, Reinhold's father, had come to the United States from Germany in 1881. After casting about in Illinois, farm and city, Gustav studied for the ministry. He was eventually assigned a parish in California, where he and his wife, Lydia, had their first two children. He was, however, a German immigrant destined for life in the Midwest, to which they soon returned. Reinhold, their third child, was born in Wright City just more than a decade after his father came to America. Thereafter, when the family moved, it would be easterly but always to small towns—first to St. Charles, closer to St. Louis; then to Lincoln, Illinois.

In Illinois, Reinhold passed his boyhood to good effect. When his father died in 1913, Reinhold was twenty, at the beginning of adult life. The father's sturdy character toughened the son's interior sense of purpose. Had Gustav lived a long life, he probably would have remained well within the Teutonic geography of the American interior. But Reinhold, heir to his father's moral culture, would obey a different conscience. He admired his father, but he set an independent course.

At the time of his father's death in April 1913, Reinhold was intent on moving east to Yale Divinity School. That fall, after spending the summer filling his father's vacant pulpit, Niebuhr made the move to Yale. There he would receive his only serious scholarly training beyond the parochial schools of his youth. The Niebuhrs, father and son, lived in times different by more than a generation. The son would be a pioneer of another kind— more restless in his way, determined to unsettle the map of America's moral geography. Reinhold's idea of *the* Church, for example, was surely aroused by his father's faithful service to local parishes. But Reinhold would serve only one parish for any length of time. His primal space was the Church universal—a spiritual dimension eerily like the American idea of space, a place everywhere in time.

Gustav Niebuhr had been a pastor in the German-speaking Evangelical Synod—a denomination of fewer than 200,000 members, most of them then in settled churches in Missouri, Illinois, and Ohio.[1] For this smallish number there were some seven hundred pastors, making the average congregation remarkably large for a day when many frontier towns could not count three hundred inhabitants. This robust ratio of pastors to communicants reflected two basic facts of church life in the near West late in the 1800s.

For one, out there pastors served as community leaders much as the Puritan divines had in the colonial era. Preachers were more, much more, than preachers. They too were frontiersmen— farmers, cowboys, even outlaws when conditions demanded. They were among the true men of their villages—closer to Clint Eastwood's preacher in *Pale Rider* than to the milquetoasts of lesser cinema. In immigrant congregations where worship and business were conducted mostly in German, the pastors were, by training and position, the ones most likely to speak English.

They were thus interpreters of the interests of the German community to the dominant English-speaking society to which they had joined their fates.

The second telling feature of church life in these frontier communities was the pastor's home—a singular institution the importance of which reached beyond a pastor's standing in the community. The parsonage, a uniquely Protestant kind of home, is an uncommonly important social institution for the nurturing of both religious and secular leaders. Growing up under the righteous gaze of a moral community instills a kind of self-awareness not well learned in domestic seclusion. The parson and his family must display a moral perfection expected but not widely practiced in the community.

Imagine the effects of the parsonage on its children. They grow up in a panopticon, a community of judges inspecting the preacher's life for flaws that might excuse their own. The preacher, as in earlier times, is meant to be the *parson*—literally *the person* who models the community's improbable standards of human conduct. Anyone able to endure childhood in the parsonage will stand up well to one of life's significant tests. Many fail. But a preacher's child who passes is likely to have learned how to be an independent yet responsible person.[2] No wonder so many leaders in various fields are preacher's kids.

This was certainly true of the Niebuhr parsonages. All three children, and a good many of *their* children, went on to leadership positions in American religious and cultural life.

Reinhold's older sister, Hulda (1889–1959), became a national leader in Christian religious education. So, too, did Reinhold's eventual wife, Ursula (1909–97), who founded the Department of Religion at Barnard College. Their daughter, Elisabeth Sifton, is one of the most respected literary editors in American publishing and author of a most wonderful book on her father's political and religious work, *Serenity Prayer: Faith and Politics in Times of Peace and War* (2003).

Reinhold's younger brother, Helmut Richard (1894–1962), became the Sterling Professor of Theology and Christian Ethics at Yale. Helmut would be known formally as H. Richard Niebuhr, author of still-classic works in the social and theological history of American religion: *Social Sources of Denominationalism* (1929), *Kingdom of God in America* (1937), and *Radical Monotheism and Western Culture* (1960).

Helmut's son and Reinhold's nephew, Richard Reinhold Niebuhr, would become the Hollis Professor of Divinity at Harvard and, like his father and uncle, one of America's influential theologians. Helmut's grandson, Gustav, was for many years a prize-winning *New York Times* religion editor before becoming a professor of journalism and religion at Syracuse University.

Parsonage upon Niebuhr parsonage turned out children who became national leaders. Yet in so distinguished a family, it was Reinhold who led American religious and political thought to new, if still unrealized, possibilities.

It is not often that one can trace so grand an adult life as Reinhold Niebuhr's to the child's family experience. Families do not determine what is to come from the child; but they can, for better or worse, set the individual on a life course. In Niebuhr's case, his life's work was a creative effort to map the unstable middle ground between social justice and individual freedom—social values that do not naturally grow in ordinary soil. Gustav and Lydia Niebuhr's small-town family in Illinois was one of the rare domestic plots in which they did.

One often repeated story of the family is of Reinhold as a boy. When his father asked him what he wanted to be when he grew up, the child said, as boys often do, that he wanted to follow in his father's footsteps—in this case to be a minister. Astonished by the seriousness, if not the originality, of the boy's response, Gustav asked why. Reinhold said, again without apparent hesitation: "Because you are the most interesting man in town."[3] Interesting, no doubt; especially in towns like those of rural Missouri and Illinois, where, I can say from personal experience, very little is interesting.

Yet what must have been more deeply interesting, apart from the father's role in the community, was Gustav's way of dealing with his children. He was, by all accounts, a strict authoritarian in the family; but also, in Reinhold's experience, a man of surprising grace. When Reinhold was but ten, Gustav surprised him by asking the boy's advice on the prospect of moving the family to a parish in Lincoln, Illinois. In German families in those days such a thing was not done. Fathers were keepers of the line meant to hold children and women to the straight and narrow. Gustav's readiness to take seriously a boy's opinion was, Reinhold would later say, a measure of the father's "passion for American egalitarianism and American freedom, which for him, meant freedom in the family."[4]

As the father, so the children—the Niebuhr family were, in their way, bred on the contradictions of their religious denomination.

They were as able to obey the strict Calvinist discipline as to enjoy the Lutheran idea of Christian liberty. By later standards, these were a strange breed of evangelical, but evangelicals they were. They were not alone among American evangelicals, but surely they stood out for their discipline in keeping faith with the two contradictory wings of Protestant Christianity.

This sort of cultural double-consciousness is encouraged in immigrant communities where the old ways and the new must somehow work together; all the more so among Germans like the Niebuhrs. Their tolerance of religious differences was consistent with their honest willingness to hold true to their German culture (then, early in the 1900s, the pinnacle of intellectual and cultural authority around the world), while at the same time taking on the new American values (then still the brash but honest values of individual freedom). Religiously, Calvinism demanded judgment (as did the Germanic culture), hence the rule of justice; Lutheran principles of spiritual liberty spawned resistance to domination (like the spirit of the American pioneers), hence the heart's openness to freedoms.

In Niebuhr's day, German-Americans were—as through much of American history—the largest group of non-English immigrants.[5] Religiously, the Germans came in all denominations. Mennonites predominated in rural Pennsylvania, Lutherans in the upper Midwest, and Catholics in the big cities. Those of the Evangelical Synod of North America (or, to be geographically precise, of the American Midwest) were unlike other German religious groups in the way they held together the opposing elements of Reformed and Lutheran thinking.

From the secular outside, this may seem to be a distinction without a difference. But historically it is a difference of religious traditions as distinct as that between the Shi'a and the Sunni—both of the same religious faiths, each with a difference as to how religious doctrines are to be understood.

Reformed Protestants are of the lineage of John Calvin (1509–64), the French theologian and founder of theocratic Geneva whose teachings led to Puritanism. Lutherans, of course, follow in the tradition of Martin Luther (1483–1546), the German priest who broke doctrinally with Roman Christianity. As Calvin's teachings led to religious dissent, Luther's led to one of the more tradition-bound of the Protestant sects. Both wings of the early Protestant movement were evangelical. Together they disestablished Roman Christendom in Europe. Each, thus, was radical in its way. But while Calvin's God was stern, he was also a god of dissent and hard work in the world. Luther's God was more generous and forgiving, but a god who meant to enforce a strict line between church and world. Thus, appearances aside, the Puritans were dissenters, hence political trouble for the authorities. The Lutherans were traditionalists, conservatives who made trouble only by accident of their religious beliefs.

Imagine, then, the improbability of a religious group like the Evangelical Synod of North America. Though smallish and remote, unlike other nineteenth-century sects this group of evangelicals kept its poise in the crosswinds of Protestant disputes. Others hunkered down in one or another doctrinal corner. Niebuhr's Evangelical Synod stood against both currents—one religiously traditional, the other dissenting. Churchgoers of this temperament are ready to tolerate substantial differences in the rules and conditions of religious life.

As time went by, the German Evangelical Synod joined in 1934 with other denominations of like disposition to become the Evangelical and Reformed (or, E and R) Church, which in time joined with the Congregational Church to become today's United Church of Christ. Naturally, through the transitions the pure contradictions of the nineteenth-century Evangelical Synod softened or fell away. Still, when the E and R merged with the Congregationalists in 1957, Niebuhr drew upon a lifetime of experience with religious differences in his own evangelical tradition to say:

> The union of the Congregational and Evangelical and Reformed churches represents ... a rather unique achievement in the history of Protestantism and not only of American Protestantism. That achievement can be most briefly designated by recalling that all previous Protestant mergers have been "family reunions"; that is, they have united or reunited churches of the same faith such as Lutherans, Methodists or Presbyterians, who had become divided by some historic contingency. This church merger unites two churches which had a different polity, theological orientation, and a different cultural history. They had little in common, in short, except the common element which ecumenical Protestantism has increasingly developed, particularly in the religious pluralism of our nation.[6]

By "cultural differences" he meant the Germanic discipline that predominated in his Evangelical and Reformed Church and the English traditions of liberty and dissent that were stronger among the Congregationalists in America.

Years later, in the 2000s, the United Church of Christ, or UCC, barely a million members and shrinking, is easily America's most liberal, even radical, mainstream Christian group. No other American denomination has been as aggressive in its pursuit of what the UCC calls open and affirming attitudes toward the politically oppressed—today gays and lesbians, as a century before the Congregationalists had been first among equals as abolitionists and, a century after that in the 1960s, leaders among civil rights activists.

In Niebuhr's youth, as today, the evangelical quest for freedoms forged on the blunt edge of social and economic justice can be overwhelmed by the easy moral fixes of American ethical individualism. Still, here and there, religious people willing to do the hard work of establishing socially just structures can be discerned in churches like those of Niebuhr's religious experience. Groups like these are among the saving remnants of the best that American liberalism could be. Inside the churches, the preaching can be as foolish and sterile as anywhere. Yet somewhere deep behind their human failings, these groups, like a goodly number of secular ones, find and keep the gospel of a better world—a social vision founded not in utopias but in the realities of this world and chastened by considered appeals to higher powers. Liberal realism, whether secular or religious, succeeds over time only so long as it practices the art of working against hard but necessary differences.

In 1915, after finishing two years of study at Yale, and but two years after his father's death, Niebuhr became the pastor of the Bethel Church in Detroit.

Nineteen fifteen was a fateful year. Europe was already at war, soon to involve the United States. America, spared the agony for a while longer, continued its rapid rise to the center of global industrial wealth. If 1914 was the end of the nineteenth century in Europe, the United States would not truly enter the realities of the twentieth century until the crash of 1929. In the fifteen-year interim, America solidified its global position among industrial powers. Only the Depression brought American down to the hard realities Europe already knew. Between 1915 and 1929 the United States enjoyed distinct economic advantages that in time would fix its ascendancy in world affairs.

Automobile manufacture was of course essential to the new industrial system—to its economic benefits and its social injustices. The Ford Motor Company was founded by Henry Ford in 1903. By the 1920s Ford had made Detroit an epicenter of global changes. Ford, the person and the firm, were then the embodiment of corporate greed sugarcoated with artificially high wages that in reality degraded working families. It did not take long after his arrival in 1915 for Niebuhr to find his way among working people in Detroit. Through them he touched the duplicitous underbelly of the modern factory system. Ford's much vaunted $5-a-day wage was, Niebuhr saw, a pittance over the long run of a year's labor. During a typical year, factories were regularly closed down for vaguely stated reasons, often for extended periods of time. In the interim no provision was made for the working families, which meant that their actual annual income was, in most cases, anything but the largess Ford claimed. Niebuhr soon took up the cause of labor.

From that beginning in Detroit, Niebuhr, still a quite young man, quickened the pace of his political work on a bewildering number of fronts. The Industrial Committee of the Detroit Council of Churches, the Federal Council of Churches, the American Association for Democratic Germany, the Bi-Racial Commission of the City of Detroit, the Highlander School in Tennessee, the Delta Cooperative Farm in Mississippi, the Council on Foreign Relations, Americans for Democratic Action, the Fellowship of Reconciliation, Freedom House, Christianity and Crisis. These were but a few of the organizations and media outlets he founded, led, or otherwise actively supported. Never merely a joiner or petition signer, Niebuhr was an activist in the full sense of the word.

When Niebuhr was a group's principal, he worked with astonishing patience, as in the case of the Delta Cooperative Farm. As president of its board of trustees, Niebuhr was brought into management of the most mundane issues—staff supervision, leasing of lands (some two thousand acres), needs of the tenant farmers, and the persistently strange demands of a fellow board member. William Amberson wrote Niebuhr obsessively from 1936 to 1939, demanding explanation of some small fiscal problem or statement of facts. Each time, Niebuhr answered in detail. It took three years for him to lose patience. Even then, he explained as best he could before saying that the more likely difficulty here was "psychiatric."[7] That seems about as severe as Niebuhr got with the hundreds who wrote him to complain about something he had said or done.

This kind of preternatural patience can come only from the deeper reserves of an interior disposition. In Niebuhr's case, patience tempered his consuming political work into a life of hard service. Moral sensibility, intellectual acuity, and energy drove Niebuhr into commitments, the sheer number of which was staggering. Whatever other faults he had, Niebuhr seemed unable to marshal his considerable energies for the long haul of life. In 1952, at sixty years of age, he suffered a debilitating stroke. Though he would live another two decades, he never recovered enough physical strength to return to the whirlwind of his earlier life. Yet Niebuhr was in time able to resume teaching and writing, and some lecturing—"from the sidelines," as he put it.[8] For most of the remaining years until his death in 1971, at age seventy-nine, Niebuhr worked as best he could with undiminished brilliance. One of his last books, *Man's Nature and His Communities* (1965, thirteen years after the stroke), is just as penetrating as the others, beginning with *Moral Man and Immoral Society* (1932, four years after his Detroit ministry).[9]

All of the work, in addition to teaching and writing, came first from the man's unusual, if ill-managed, moral and physical energy. Yet it seems unlikely that it would have poured forth with such a force had he not been chastened by direct confrontation with the economic injustices of the capitalist order. The Detroit years are rightly considered the key to Niebuhr's life and work—not for any one aspect but for the total experience. Pastoral and political work against stark injustices brought home the realization that when one trusts reliable conviction, thinks deeply, and works as hard any one person can, things can change for the better. This is not a lesson easily learned by the young.

It is learned, if at all, in the day-by-day push and pull of political exertion.

Niebuhr kept a journal of his years in the Detroit parish, later published, with heavy editing, as *Leaves from the Notebook of a Tamed Cynic* (1929). *Leaves* reveals quite a lot about the young minister's finer qualities of character.

At the start of his parish career, Niebuhr was but twenty-three years old. Young men can be particularly foolish when they find themselves called to serve people many years their elder, armed with little more than what they learned in childhood and were taught in schools. Few who have not tried it can have any idea how exhausting this work can be. Not least are the burdens of the now largely abandoned practice of pastoral calls upon the homes of parishioners. Before the time of the culture of fear, the pastor would appear unannounced at a home—there to perform some ill-defined pastoral service. Niebuhr said of the experience in his first year in the parish:

> I am glad that there are only eighteen families in this church. I have been visiting the members for six weeks and haven't seen all of them yet. Usually I walk past a house two or three times before I summon the courage to go in. I am always very courteously received, so I don't know exactly why I should not be able to overcome this curious timidity. I don't know that very much comes out of my visits except that I really get acquainted with the people. . . . Usually after I have made a call I find some excuse to quit for the afternoon. (1915)[10]

The exhaustion comes from a desire—more pronounced among boys—to be someone who is expected to bring something to the course of events. The priest with his ecclesiastical regalia and office can bring the Church into those homes. The Protestant minister, with his plain shirt, brings only himself and the charge that he is meant, somehow, to cause something good to happen; and this with the family dog sniffing at his crotch.

If wise, as Niebuhr was, the young minister learns to accept the limitations, which are nowhere more exposed than when preaching.

> There is something ludicrous about a callow young fool like myself standing up to preach a sermon to these good folks. I talk wisely about life and know little about life's problems. I tell them of the need for sacrifice, although most of them could tell me something about what that really means. (1915)[11]

Niebuhr, however, did not succumb to self-doubt.

Even before he came to see the evil of the industrial order, World War I taught him a lesson that would be at the foundation of his preaching and teaching in later years.

> I can see one element in this strange fascination of war which men have not adequately noted. It reduces life to simple terms. The modern man lives in such a complex world that one wonders how his sanity is maintained as well as it is. Every moral venture, every social situation and every practical problem involves a whole series of conflicting loyalties, and a man may never be quite sure that he is right in giving himself to the one as against the other. (1918)[12]

By 1923, eight years into his tenure in the Detroit parish, Niebuhr's journal reveals how quickly and surely his thinking had moved away from the moral individualism then prevalent in American Protestantism and toward a social theory of the moral failures of modern societies. Niebuhr came to realize that the relation between individual morality and the structures of the social world is perverse:

> In one sense modern civilization substitutes unconscious sin of more destructive consequences for conscious sins of less destructive consequences. Men try consciously to eliminate the atrocities of society, but meanwhile they unheedingly build a civilization which is more destructive of moral and personal values than anything intended in a more primitive society. (1923)[13]

One might suppose that meditations like this came from the cynic who would be tamed. But the 1920s in America were still, for the most part, a time of innocence when cynicism, such as it was, was tamer than it would be in later years.

In those days, an important influence on liberal parish ministers like Niebuhr was the Social Gospel movement—a religious tradition among Protestants that grew out of the Progressive Era of the late nineteenth century. Pastors like Washington Gladden (1836–1918), a Congregational minister in Columbus, Ohio, and Walter Rauschenbusch (1861–1918), a Baptist minister with a formative experience in Hell's Kitchen in New York City, addressed their writing and pastoral work to the social problems of a modernizing nation. In words that Niebuhr himself would in time echo, Rauschenbusch put the issue simply: "The social gospel is the old message of salvation, but enlarged and intensified. The individualistic gospel has taught us to see the sinfulness of every human heart and has inspired us with faith in the willingness of power of God to save every soul that comes to him. But it has not given us an adequate understanding of the sinfulness of the social order and its share in the sins of all individuals within it."[14] Without throwing off the evangelical spirit of American Protestantism, the Social Gospel movement rallied religious and secular reformers to move beyond individualist pieties and attack the social sins of the modern order. They were, in effect, religious sociologists at a time when, in America, academic sociology was at best ill-formed.

Still, the Social Gospel was utopian in the liberal sense of proclaiming that historical progress was on the side of the good. "There is no inherent contradiction whatever," wrote Rauschenbusch, "between the hope of progressive development of mankind toward the Kingdom of God and the hope of the consummation of our personal life in an existence after death."[15] Where there is unwarranted hope in human progress, there is also a pious heart—nowhere more so than in the words of Washington Gladden's familiar hymn:

> In hope that sends a shining ray
> Far down the future's broadening way,
> In peace that only Thou canst give,
> With Thee, O Master, let me live.[16]

Niebuhr described this way of thinking as perfectionist—that is: committed to a perfect kingdom in this world, and trusting that man was good enough to bring it about. Just the same, the Social Gospel activists staked the first serious claim in twentieth-century America for religion as a social force—as, thereby, much more than a healing balm to the souls of individuals.

The Social Gospel movement began to fade in the early 1920s, but it had had a chastening effect on young ministers like

Niebuhr, who were stationed in the burgeoning industrial cities where only the hard of heart could ignore the human signs of modern capitalism's selfish greed. Niebuhr would not long remain under the influence of this sort of liberal thinking; but it undoubtedly touched him to the core in these early years in Detroit.[17]

For Niebuhr, 1926 was a crucial year in his political work. The American Federation of Labor (AFL) held its annual convention in Detroit. As is the custom when an important group is in town, local churches had offered their halls as venues for speakers from the AFL. But Detroit's corporate leaders exerted pressure to close down the pro-labor meetings. Churches that had agreed to open their doors to the labor speakers were forced to withdraw their invitations, as did the YMCA when Henry Ford threatened to withhold his $1.5 million building program pledge. Others folded under the weight of their own cowardice. Only Niebuhr's Bethel Church and one other refused to cave in. A sign of his strength as a pastor was that the parish went along with his wishes, facing up to the city's corporate interests. Lukewarm liberals are bottom-liners, worried more about survival than duty. Niebuhr had already taken his parish with him beyond this sort of tepid thinking.

Nineteen twenty-six was near the end of Niebuhr's ministry in Detroit. From his first years there, more than a decade before, his influence in the city had grown steadily. In the Detroit years he deepened the habit of working late into the night writing newspaper columns, letters, and magazine articles. Steady and probative, he had become a national figure noted for stingingly well-reasoned criticism of the overreaching social evil of modern industrial society and of modern civilization, as he called it in those days. Somehow all this came forth at the end of long days attending to parish duties but increasingly leading and organizing the city's church fathers on the side of exploited workers.

The better known he became, the more he traveled and wrote. Weekends he preached on college campuses. Regularly he contributed to the pages of the (then liberal) *Christian Century*. Soon enough he was traveling abroad—notably visiting Europe with other Christian leaders to investigate the devastating effects of the world war, especially in Germany, where the punitive Versailles Treaty of 1919 had led to suffering and hardship and much more. During the Detroit years he would shed what remained of the utopian ideals that came naturally to liberal preachers and quite a few illiberal ones. The pattern of his life had become fixed by the habits of travel, writing, preaching—of plain old hard work that wore him down. Only the stroke in 1952 slowed him down.

Most important, the key themes of his contributions to political and religious thought had begun to take shape in Detroit. In the concluding journal entry in *Leaves from the Notebook a Tamed Cynic*, he wrote:

Modern industry, particularly American industry, is not Christian. The economic forces which move it are hardly qualified at a single point by really ethical considerations. If, while it is in the flush of its early triumphs, it may seem impossible to bring it under the restraint of moral law, it may strengthen faith to know that life without law destroys itself. If the church can do nothing else, it can bear witness to the truth until such a day as bitter experience will force a recalcitrant civilization to a humility which it does not now possess. (1928)[18]

This was 1928—the year Walt Disney introduced Mickey Mouse. In bourgeois America, it was still the Age of Jazz and *Gatsby*. The blush was still on the rose of America's late passing nineteenth-century culture. Niebuhr's words cut deep—almost inconceivably sharp for such a time. A year later came the crash that would change the world.

Niebuhr was never truly a cynic, nor was he tamed by the terrible economic events. Already in 1929 a realist, he realized that moral and political engagements always came with the temptation to think too highly of one's principles. "It is no easy task," he said when *Leaves* appeared in 1929, "to deal realistically with the moral confusion of our day, either in the pulpit or the pew, and avoid the appearance, and possibly the actual peril, of cynicism."[19] The book's title was thus ironic. In taming himself against the risk of cynicism, Niebuhr opened the way for the life to follow—a life anything but tame in respect to the cynical injustices of industrial America.

In 1928 Niebuhr left Detroit to accept a teaching post at the Union Theological Seminary in New York City. There he would become and remain an active force in the nation's most dynamic, global city, and in the nation as a whole.

One telling indication of his readiness for the larger challenge is a letter written to him on April 30, 1928, by John C. Dancy, head of the Detroit Urban League:

Through the columns of the daily papers I am apprised of your taking leave from Detroit to enter the teaching field in another city. Had this news come mentioning some other minister it would perhaps have occasioned not a syllable from me, but in your case that is something else again. I do not speak for myself only. I feel that I am expressing the feelings and sentiments of the great majority of Negroes in Detroit, when I say that there is genuine regret in the minds of the colored group of this city at your leave taking. There are many of us still mindful of your usefulness in trying to do those things which would mean for better understanding and better relationships between the races in the city of Detroit. To have you go without an expression of our appreciation of your services would be rank ingratitude.[20]

Nineteen twenty-eight in America was the year the *Amos 'n' Andy* radio program premiered—with whites reading the black roles. Few whites earned such praise from the other side of the color line. The one who did could no longer be contained by local affairs.

What Niebuhr had done in Detroit was, however, just the beginning. He was already well beyond his times. He required a more worldly setting for what was to come.

2
evangelical preacher

wheat and tares

In Detroit, from 1915 to 1928, Niebuhr had established himself as more than a pastor. His national reputation as a political analyst was already strong when he left for Union Theological Seminary in New York. His admirers in Detroit were not surprised that he had been drawn away. But when he began his career as a seminary teacher in New York, it was far from evident that Reinhold Niebuhr would become an enduring figure in the history of twentieth-century America. Many of the faculty at Union Seminary were not even certain that he was qualified to join their distinguished academic ranks.

Yet even before his reputation as a thinker of abiding ideas was recognized, it was possible to identify the rough outlines of his life's work in the hectic years in the Detroit parish. If there is one question, then and now, that American society has yet to ask and answer, it would be: How, if at all, can democracies serve both individual liberties and social justice? No question is more basic. None less well attended to; few so loftily proclaimed and practically difficult to achieve. Yet no one in America until then had done as much as Niebuhr—and few have since—to clarify the terms of the dilemma and point to the kind of solution required.

Niebuhr's work after Detroit, though political and pastoral, forced him to set aside the simpler ideas of democracy he had experienced in the home and churches of his rural childhood. Detroit was a different America in which the hard injustices of industrial life cut to the quick of any responsible moral soul. Detroit and the false promises of Henry Ford's calculating management of the production line forced the young pastor to reevaluate the liberal religious ideas learned at Yale, as well as the inadequacy of Social Gospel liberalism that in the 1920s inspired socially conscious church people. Yet as Niebuhr himself moved with determined purpose away from liberalism as a generic political philosophy, his ideas and commitments drew more and more liberals to his side.[1] The wise among them, however, saw even in the early years in New York City that Reinhold Niebuhr, no longer a cynic, not even a mere skeptic, was inventing a full-bodied social ethic strong enough to pull America away from its innocence and toward a realistic social ethic.

Decades later, in 2007, one of America's most dogged social liberals, Arthur Schlesinger, Jr., who had known and admired Niebuhr since their political work in the 1940s, wrote of the need for a reconsideration of Reinhold Niebuhr's Christian realism:

> Niebuhr was a critic of national innocence, which he regarded as a delusion. After all, whites coming to these shores were reared in the Calvinist doctrine of sinful humanity, and they killed red men, enslaved black men, and later on imported yellow men for peon labor—not much of a background of national innocence. "Nations, as individuals, who are completely innocent in their own esteem," Niebuhr wrote, "are insufferable in their human contacts." The self-righteous delusion of innocence encouraged a kind of Manichaeism dividing the world between good (us) and evil (our critics).[2]

Like Niebuhr, Schlesinger lived to experience the Cold War, a modern archetype of good-versus-evil thinking. Unlike Niebuhr (who died in 1971), Schlesinger (who died in 2007) lived to witness the terrible innocence of American foreign policy after the events of September 11, 2001.

Yet decades after Niebuhr's death, 9/11 reminds us just how hard it is to grasp serious evil. For Niebuhr, the Nazi reign of terror was the paradigmatic historical evil. Deeper still, his theory of human evil was religious in origin and character while at the same time allowing for evil as an aspect of the human situation. He moved well beyond commonly popular religious ideas by understanding evil to be a historical reality that overrode naïve Manichean ideologies. Since ancient times, the Manichean principle that the cosmos was subject to the battle between a divine good struggling with a comparably powerful evil force appealed to those who lived with historical tragedies while hoping for the good to triumph. With rare exceptions across the length and breadth of history, high religious doctrine determining political ideologies supposed that one nation or empire embodies the good in a struggle against evil enemies.

Religions are vulnerable to foolish pieties—the feeling or doctrine that they alone can discern the superior goodness of the actions and beliefs they themselves espouse. But piety itself is a generically human attitude that far outruns its religious origins. Whether weak or strong, secular ideologies can lapse into Manichean piety for which the only sure antidote is a serious engagement with realities of the daily grind. What impressed even secular liberals in Niebuhr's day was that his ideas were forged in hard political work and, though unembarrassedly born of his religious life as a preacher and teacher, they were utterly devoid of pious swagger.

What began in Detroit blossomed in New York as Niebuhr balanced the life of a teacher and scholar in one of America's most distinguished schools of Protestant theology with the work of a political commentator and leader immersed in Left politics in America and abroad. Lesser individuals would not have even realized that the two lives could be fused. Niebuhr did as few others before and since have.

In the 1930s the global Depression was at its worst and thus unavoidably also a question of economic justice. Franklin Delano Roosevelt's presidency from 1932 to 1945 was the one extended period in American political history when, directly and indirectly, a strong social program of economic fairness dominated the political scene. Would the United States have overcome the Depression without Roosevelt? Would England have survived German aggression without the United States and the alliance between Churchill and Roosevelt? These are questions of virtual history for which there can be no answer. What is known is that, in the long travail from 1929 to 1945, FDR set the table for any and all serious programs for economic and military progress. And the table Roosevelt set, against the instincts of his own wealthy upper-class upbringing, was one of social justice for the collective good. His was not a social philosophy of the rights of righteous individuals.

Today there are still those who hate what they call anti-American "socialism"; and their hatred is rooted in the plutocratic loathing of Roosevelt's social programs—Social Security, public work projects, support for artist and teachers, income support, and other welfare benefits. Those programs and that era were exceptional in America's political history. From its independent beginnings early in the nineteenth century, American public philosophy was an ideology of individual freedoms and rights. Except in times of war and civil strife, Americans normally clear the political decks of any serious programs of social justice. The 1930s were, then, the crucible in which Reinhold Niebuhr forged his own social ethic by taking up the underlying dilemma of American politics: How can a nation built on a culture of individualisms also come to terms with the collective demands of social and economic justice? The dilemma is not one of mere ideological preferences. The political double bind of American public ethics is that individual rights are relatively cheap, while social justice is expensive. The costs of collective action are seen as threats to the free market of economic progress. The United States is not alone with this dilemma, but it is unique in the extent to which it binds hard the goodwill of its people.

Democracies have to be pushed to the extreme to think of the collective good. They will, to be sure, fight wars (some of them foolish) in the name of rights and freedoms, all the while depleting their accounts of the funds that could have paid for enough economic justice to have made at least some wars unnecessary. Otherwise, and especially in America, the dilemma, even when it is ignored, is based on the inherent tensions between high moral ideals and hard economic injustices. And on this basic issue, Niebuhr struck a chord in his day because he understood, as he put it, the irony of American history.[3] No other modern society has so boasted of its democratic principles while so severely denying them to its own people. In the United States, in contrast to Europe, rights and freedoms have long drowned out appeals for social and economic justice. The long history of the social failure of modern societies confirms just how fragile freedoms are when not supported by tangible social fairness. The poor are often too weak to flee. They may have just enough strength to dig in their heels. Social justice gives them traction. Liberal or not, a fair society might even be good for business. Fairness certainly encourages inclusion, which is good for community.

Niebuhr surely is on the short list of twentieth-century thinkers who addressed the dilemma of democratic social order;

and he heads the list of those who drew deeply from the American preoccupation with religion in order to challenge America's tardiness—even refusal—to repair its own injustices. The United States takes pride, much of it deserved, in its commitment to democratic institutions. What Niebuhr understood was that behind the pride is the social sin of institutions that in the long run undercut democratic realities for those millions excluded from a fair share of the nation's enormous wealth. Though a preacher and teacher of religious values, Niebuhr stands nearly alone as an honest broker of the political and social promises of religious ideas.

In the long run, Niebuhr's social teachings, appealing as they were to the secular left, never would have come to light had it not been for his evangelical faith and practice. And nowhere is that faith more typically practiced than in preaching. Still, Reinhold Niebuhr was first and foremost the preacher, but somehow a preacher who was not preachy; and especially not when addressing any of the predominantly secular audiences to which he often spoke. The following is one of many reports of Niebuhr's powerful effect against the odds of late-night weariness among such a gathering:

> The final speaker was introduced. No one in the crowded dinning room seemed to pay much attention. It was Saturday night in the Spring of 1949, and several hundred politically minded people had been in that Chicago hotel for thirty-six hours trying to hammer out recommendations for improving the nation's foreign and domestic policy. By ten o'clock the air was stale and the people were stale. The

stimulating effect of the cocktail hour had worn away, leaving a glaze in the eye, a weight on the limbs, and an irresistible desire to yawn. A young couple from New York noted with relief that the final speaker carried no prepared text.

The speaker straightened his tie, ran a big-knuckled hand over his shiny pate, pulled his long nose further downward, and spoke out rapidly in a deep voice. By the end of one sentence, he had every person's full attention; by the end of one hour, he had several hundred people on their feet, clapping, stamping, shouting their approval.

Few speeches can have rivaled this one for profundity, for range, for electromagnetism. Listeners sat bolt upright, their fists clenched, as the speaker bombarded them with startling new ideas, startling interpretations of old ideas, dramatic challenges to their long-accepted presuppositions, and sudden explosive humor.[4]

The audience probably comprised men and women of the political left, more than likely a meeting of Americans for Democratic Action—lefties not known for their religious devotion. Whether from a pulpit or a lectern, Niebuhr's magic arose from his brilliance, yes, but also from his willingness to engage the unvarnished realities in ways that those gathered understood without having quite thought of them as he did.

Niebuhr's ability to speak powerfully to crowds of all kinds was uncanny. He could just as readily hold in thrall university students as farmers in rural churches or workers and executives in Detroit or theologians and ministers at Union Theological Seminary or in Europe. He was many things to many people. Many who would never darken the door of a church knew Niebuhr to be one of the most influential political thinkers and leaders of their time. To this day there are those who think of themselves as "Atheists for Niebuhr"—a half-in-jest tag invented in his lifetime.[5] Yet it is plain that Niebuhr's gifts as a speaker grew out of his evangelical faith and his preaching.

When Niebuhr was slowed by a stroke in 1952, it was well before the era of televangelism. When he died in 1971, evangelical megachurches were fewer in number and less prominent in the public sphere. Niebuhr was not an evangelical in the corrupt sense into which the term has declined in our day. His was truer by far to the honest meaning of evangelical faith—closer by a decent measure to the emerging social-justice evangelicals who began to assert themselves early in the 2000s.[6]

Evangelical, literally, means "of or pertaining to the gospels." Before all else, an evangelical is usually a Protestant who recognizes the four gospels of Christian Scripture as the source and authority of faith. Those for whom religion is at best a puzzle, like those who might be appalled, as Niebuhr would have been, by the evangelicals who darken the screen of public life early in the twenty-first century, are likely to be more puzzled still by the convergence of intellectual and spiritual forces in Niebuhr's unique contributions to public life in America.

In principle, all of the many varieties of Christian religious traditions are evangelical. Christian belief depends on the story of Jesus of Nazareth. That story has been described by the literary critic Harold Bloom (himself not in the least Christian) as one of the great stories in world literature.[7] Still, as powerful as it may be among adherents, the Jesus story has been variously understood among the multitude of incongruous forms of Christian religious thinking and practice. Was Jesus a man of special wisdom? Was he the Son of God? Was he both? Were his miracles signs of his divine powers? Or were they evidences of the man's ability to inspire those who heard him? Did his death and resurrection redeem the world? Or was his death a compelling example of human virtue? These are but some of the questions that run through the countless denominations of the world's largest religion, eroding the common ground. For Niebuhr the contestations were, if not tragic, an abiding distraction from the essential evangelical message that he summarized in one place as "the experience of grace" or "the apprehension of the absolute from the perspective of the relative."[8]

Among Christians of all kinds, their differences abounding, it is the Protestants who are normally the evangelicals. In his teaching at Union Seminary over the years, Niebuhr was consistently respectful, but also astutely critical, of all Christian theologies, Protestant no less than Catholic. Yet Niebuhr's personal history as a preacher and religious thinker was evidence that he could not but defend the Protestant position, whatever its many perversions, for its steady reliance on what Protestants, more than others, call "the Gospel."

The Gospel is not the same as the *gospels*—the first four books of what the Christians call their New Testament. These books, attributed to the apostles Mark, Luke, Matthew, and John, are fundamental to the faith. Whether they are the only true accounts of the life and sayings of Jesus is far from clear. They do not even tell the same story. The shortest, the Gospel According to Mark, is generally agreed to have been the earliest and the sourcebook for Luke's and Matthew's accounts. John's story is latest, and very different from the other three in being more philosophical, more Greek than Jewish.

Plus which, between the true stories of Jesus and the story of the early Church the line is far from settled. The Acts of the Apostles, thought to be of the same source as the Gospel According to Luke, is roughly the story of the early Church. It introduces Saul of Tarsus, the notorious persecutor of Christians who converted to the faith to be become St. Paul, the missionary to the Greek and Roman worlds. Paul's pastoral letters to the Christian communities he visited are the most reliable, if scanty, account of life in the young churches in the years after Jesus was executed. Many theologians, Niebuhr among them, took Paul's teachings (especially his pastoral letter to the Christians at Rome) as not just a true reflection on the Gospel, but a powerful development after the death of Jesus of its implications for Christian life.[9]

Still, the main theme of *the Gospel* turns on who Jesus was, what he did, and what he promised. The whole thing is open to countless interpretations, which have led to as many churches or sects formed in the name of one or another of those interpretations. In principle, the message is always the Gospel of Good News that Jesus did something for or to us—something that offers hope at a price.

The Protestant medium for this message is the sermon—a remarkably flimsy ritual for such an important story, nonetheless an apt conveyance for a narrative so resistant to a single intelligible plot. One of the historical mysteries of Christianity is how so small a minority sect in a remote corner of the Roman Empire would, first, provoke the powerful Romans to suppress it; then, in time (324 C.E.), become not only the official religion of the Empire but ultimately (800 C.E.), when the Holy Roman Empire picked up the pieces of fallen Rome, the administrative agency of medieval Europe. Once the medieval Church had become a wealthy and powerful force, rival to the royal families, the mystery fell away. It was a moment, according to Niebuhr, when Christianity gave away its soul. His was not a mindless anti-Catholic bias but a judgment drawn from a theory of history he would develop late in the 1930s. For Niebuhr, as for uncorrupted evangelical Protestants generally, the mystery of Christianity's ability to endure against the odds was resuscitated in the Reformation in the sixteenth century. For Protestants mystery is of the essence. Yet religious reasons aside, the sociology of the mystery pertains to the demonstrably feeble medium Protestants rely on for the declamation of the Gospel.

Preaching requires a message, but it also must have a rhetorical form. For high church Christians that form is the ritual culminating in the Eucharist. For most Protestant sects, it is the sermon—which normally follows the only formula there is for broadcasting a message of this sort: *Jesus did X for you; you must therefore do Y, if you want the benefits of X.*

As in all things Protestant, there is room for confusion as to the *X*s and the *Y*s, of which the most prominent is the question of whether a believer can do any *Y* if the *X* done by Jesus was to inform us that God loves us unconditionally. A gift given must never be returned in kind unless by prior agreement (in which case it is not a gift but a barter, and one does not barter with the gods). When it comes to the gifts of the Protestant gods, not only *must* one not give them back in kind, one *cannot*.

Inasmuch as any and all religions are, strictly speaking, meant to bind their adherents to a higher power, the problem all religion entails is that believers want the power on their own terms. The Protestant gospel thus could be said to be the perfect religion in that it keeps the faithful guessing.[10] Yet the faithful are human, and they are easily seduced by false prophets, wondrous icons, fancy gowns, miraculous healings, and all the other amazing stuff you can see late at night on the channels you'd never watch had you not drunk too much.

So long as he was able to be active, Niebuhr thought of himself as an itinerant preacher. When he retired from Union in 1960, he said he was sorry that his "ministry" had come to an end. From 1915 until then, he had accepted invitations to fill pulpits, when he could, mostly on college campuses, most weekends (and this before jet travel). Preaching was part of who he was, and he did it extraordinarily well. So much so that, in a long conversation with Karl Barth, the Swiss neo-orthodox theologian with whom Niebuhr is often misidentified, he shocked the great man when he responded to a point of theological interpretation by saying that he was "too much a preacher not to look for points of contact between the truth of the Gospel and the despair of the world."[11]

But also, you might say that evangelical preaching was effectively what Niebuhr did in more ways than the apparent one. Listen to the several hundred of his recorded public talks, academic lectures, and sermons available today and it is hard to distinguish among them in tone and substance. Niebuhr's public speaking was, as witnesses confirm, direct. He spoke with no more than a few notes, filled with factual and intellectual detail, presented in a dramatic style that kept those present riveted; and above all they were clear: "I think even his voice made the difficulties clear. He sounded like what he had been to start with, a young parson in a community of German-speaking farmers in southern Illinois, so that plain Middle Western, middle American speech had a hint of the kinder vowels and rhythmic intensity you get in the South, along with a certain German precision and majesty."[12] Yet he was not a showman. He could surprise with an occasional joke, a sudden change in tempo, an amazing juxtaposition of ideas—but the presentation itself was always bound tight by Niebuhr's seriousness of purpose.

If Niebuhr had been forced to select only one sermon as the one way to put *the Way*—the Wheat and the Tares probably would have been it. In fact, few texts recur so regularly over his life, from the earliest years in the Detroit parish to the latter years. Those who knew him best commonly selected this one sermon or ones like it to illustrate his preaching at its best.[13]

Another parable put he forth unto them, saying, The kingdom of heaven is likened unto a man which sowed good seed in his field: But while men slept, his enemy came and sowed tares among the wheat, and went his way. But when the blade was sprung up, and brought forth fruit, then appeared the tares also. So the servants of the householder came and said unto him, Sir, didst not thou sow good seed in thy field? from whence then hath it tares? He said unto them, An enemy hath done this. The servants said unto him, Wilt thou then that we go and gather them up? But he said, Nay; lest while ye gather up the tares, ye root up also the wheat with them. Let both grow together until the harvest: and in the time of harvest I will say to the reapers, Gather ye together first the tares, and bind them in bundles to burn them: but gather the wheat into my barn. (Matthew 13:24–30)

This parable, like most of those attributed to Jesus, well illustrates the preacher's dilemma. When free to choose a text, as liturgically informal Protestants are, why choose one like this? Any reasonable preacher would know in advance that even an attentive layperson might say of it: What the hell? And what are tares?

Niebuhr's reason for the choice would have been determined not by the superficial appeal of the story but by the hard truth of its point. He might begin, "This story is of course very bad agricultural theory."[14] There was always a laugh, if only because even a city slicker knows that farming, like gardening, is all about pulling up weeds that choke the bounty. Parables, more perhaps than any other literary form, depend on irony. They present as allegory or metaphor, "The kingdom of heaven may be compared to a man who sowed good seed in his field." But they quickly turn on the surprise in the comparison.

"Sir, did you not sow good seed in your field? How then has it weeds?" He said to them, "An enemy has done this." The servants said to him, "Then do you want us to go and gather them?" But he said, "No; lest in gathering the weeds you root up the wheat along with them. Let both grow together until the harvest; and at harvest time I will tell the reapers, Gather the weeds first and bind them in bundles to be burned, but gather the wheat into my barn."

The truth, if known at all, is in the harvest beyond time.

Like most religious parables, this one turns the tables on normal expectations. Irony seizes attention by a cunning reversal. At some level one could say that the Gospel itself is ironic. The story is that things are not what they seem: *Death is life; life is short in human time but long in God's time; the first will be last, the last first.* Here, in the parable of the Wheat and the Tares, all these ingredients are packed together into a black hole of wisdom.

Life is impossibly brief, like the growing season: "In the morning it flourisheth, and groweth up; in the evening it is cut down, and withereth" (Psalms 90:6).[15] The harvest comes too soon. All the careful weeding of the tares is futile—not because the weeds are as good as the wheat, but because from any point in human history it is impossible to know for certain which is the good wheat and which the evil weed. In other words, from within the limits of human history, you can never be sure who or what is good. Let the weeds grow. Time is short. The final harvest is not yours to make.

To take to heart parables like the Wheat and the Tares, one must have already accepted the religious idea that life is short, as obviously it is. But even more difficult for those who like to know life's truths, one must accept that the outcome of human life is not ours to know. Where Niebuhr's sermon cuts to the quick is by bringing the righteous up short. Having chosen regularly to attend a service of Christian worship, they come inclined to think of themselves as God's righteous wheat. Yet if the message is taken with full seriousness, they are as likely to be weeds. You bother with church because you admit something is missing in your life; once there, you want to trust that the mere going is sufficient unto righteousness, which confidence mocks the true nature of any honest religion. Niebuhr concludes the sermon with this larger point—always, as here, with a political aspect:

> Thus human history is a mixture of wheat and tares. We must make provisional distinctions, but we must know that there are no final distinctions. "Let both grow together until the harvest." Man is a creature and a creator. He would not be a creator, if he could not overlook the human scene and be able to establish goals beyond those of nature and to discriminate between good and evil. He must do these things. But he must also remember that no matter how high his creativity may rise, he is himself involved in the flow of time, and he becomes evil at the precise point where he pretends not to be, where he pretends his wisdom is not finite, but infinite, and his virtue not ambiguous but unambiguous.[16]

Strictly speaking, one does not preach the Gospel. It is a story that cannot be spelled out so much as proclaimed. Good news is gossip to be passed on. It is not reasoned truth. Faith is taking it in, for better or worse, without defiant skepticism. All manner of trouble can be made when gossip is passed along—and that, implicitly, is the point Niebuhr makes. Who are we to think we know how to distinguish the evil from the good? We must wait, and trust.

This, again, is the point Protestant Christianity emphasizes when at its best. The essential act of worship is the proclamation of the good news before witnesses who may or may not quite get the point. As a result, the Gospel is always proclaimed in the presence but over the heads of the gathered faithful. Faith cannot be proven or measured, save in God's time.

John Wesley (1703–91), the founder of Methodism, is known to have preached thousands upon thousands of sermons. He is reported to have once said that, of them all, there were only six messages. Actually he exaggerated. There is only one message, however many themes and nuances may convey it. Crudely put that one message would be: *You never know. Jesus is the Way.* What it is that is never known is by definition unknown. How Jesus is *the Way*, and what *the Way* might be, are similarly inscrutable, thus open to the endless variations. This is what makes Protestant Christianity so maddening, and inclines many varieties of Protestants to make so much trouble. They don't know what they are talking about because they cannot.

Evangelical Protestantism is thus a sectarian religion in that the core of the faith is eschatological—that is, rooted in the early gospels when followers of Jesus defined themselves as people waiting for the Messiah to return and the world to end. Needless to say, Christianity had to adjust to the reality that no End came in the early days or has come since. But even as the early Christians organized themselves into enduring churches fit for this world, the failure of the original expectation did not cause them to make less trouble, not even, centuries later, after the Protestant Reformation attempted to revive the original purity of the earliest Christians. Waiting for something big can lead to the damnedest things.

Niebuhr's understanding of the Gospel was orthodox or, in the expression of his day, neo-orthodox—a label that misleads so many of his interpreters. It might better be said that his orthodoxy was notably heterodox. Niebuhr's neo-orthodoxy refers most directly to the way he jettisoned the plain liberalism of his Detroit years. This was, however, a relative departure. Niebuhr's orthodoxy, by whichever name, was original to his years as a teacher of social ethics in New York City. In the years after leaving the Midwest to settle in the East, his thinking—hence his politics—moved decisively toward what might be called a general theory of sin. Hence in the first place, he was orthodox in the sense of rejecting the liberal idea that all things are possible. But there is more.

For the unwashed (literally, those not baptized), *sin* is a term to be avoided except as a caricature of the worst that can come from religious enthusiasm. For Niebuhr, sin meant something much more profound than the mindless denunciation of evil in the human spirit. Sin, put all too simply (but not, I think, over-simply), was for him the universal human *in*ability to recognize human limitations—to admit that as much as we know, or think we know, we do not and cannot know the final truth of life. Sin is more, to say it precisely, the species arrogance that is very well exaggerated in the modern age that will not allow us to know that we do not know. Sin is an essential selfishness—or self-preoccupation—that breeds pride and arrogance.

What distinguishes Niebuhr from other orthodox and neo-orthodox theologians is that his seriousness as to the sin of cultural arrogance did not prevent him from appreciating the creative freedom and power of the human spirit. The Gospel, for Niebuhr, was not hellfire and damnation as punishment for humankind's errant ways. It was, for him, an irony, of which the most subtle expressions were parables like the Wheat and the Tares. *Humans know, but they do not know that they cannot know the essential thing.* Our freedom and capacity for knowledge moves us not to humility of spirit and moral responsibility but back unto our selves—to, that is, the norms of a pure unbridled self. The only important knowledge, in spiritual terms, Niebuhr would come to say, is this: *Humans are the only creatures who have knowledge of themselves, thus also the only creatures capable of using this knowledge to destroy themselves.* We know we are naked; yet we reach for the apple that spoils the party. The human dilemma thus is in not being able to know the difference between what can be known, or done, and what cannot.

It is strange today to speak of "man." Since Niebuhr's death in 1971, the ungendered innocence of the word has been exposed. Yet the gender insensitivities of earlier days being granted, even an enormously sympathetic man like Niebuhr (who today would find a way around the clumsiness of the unglossed term *man*) would have been drawn to it, as others were, because of the incongruities devolving from the paradox of an unknowable personal god who makes claims on human history.

Then, as now, to speak of "sin" is for many the greater linguistic offense. They in turn indulge a more subtle foolishness. To reduce the mysteries of life to science, or historical seriousness, or intellectual rigor is to slaughter what truths might be born only in the inscrutable.[17] No sensible religious thinker would deny that religion is a very human thing—thus vulnerable to all the common frailties of the species. To speak of human failure is one thing. To speak of the poetry of man's relation to the gods is another. Hence, language aside, the foundational theme of the Wheat and the Tares sermon:

> Man is a creature and a creator. He would not be a creator, if he could not overlook the human scene and be able to establish goals beyond those of nature and to discriminate between good and evil. He must do these things. But he must also remember that no matter how high his creativity may rise, he is himself involved in the flow of time, and he becomes evil at the precise point where he pretends not to be, where he pretends his wisdom is not finite, but infinite, and his virtue not ambiguous but unambiguous.

"Man is a creature and creator." He may well be. As often as not he is a she. Either way, she or he is a responsible party to human history. Her finitude is defined by her infinitude. She is a compound being, an actor, and thereby an actor who cannot achieve all that she can imagine. Man is both creator and creature—both at once, thus neither necessarily. As creator he knows that to know is in his nature. As creature, he can know what is known only by the gods—the knowledge of good and evil, which, in the end, amounts to the ultimate practical knowledge: Am I wheat or weed? If the latter, what am I to do to become wheat? The sermon is the means and relative medium of a message of an absolute that cannot be fully explained.

As Niebuhr grew into his theological maturity in New York City, he became what is known as a Christian realist—a philosophical position related to, but different from, philosophical realism, which is more concerned with the status of ideas and concepts. Niebuhr was a realist, to be sure, about the religious ideas that informed his thinking. But he was just as much a political realist in the rather limited sense of always, without exception, seeking to locate man, so to speak, in human history, and locating her with respect to the strengths and weaknesses of that history. Here, then, is where Niebuhr's religious thinking was informed by his understandings of social realities.

Unlike the Social Gospel theologians, Niebuhr did not begin with social things. He began always, if you want to call it this way, with his theory of human frailty—as creature and creator; neither one nor the other absolutely. How else is one to make sense of this kind of thinking if not by reference to a book of sacred stories that offer up the Gospel story that can be taken only on its own terms? There is no Gospel if man is unambiguously able to know the whys and wherefores of what she creates. Bear a child; do your best; the kid turns out as he will turn out. In the end, religious realism is about knowing what can be known, accepting what cannot be known, and living *in* the difference. There is no other way to a just Kingdom. Rights allow one to live. But justice arises only when those living together realize that they live in the same inscrutable boat.

3
powers, pulpits, and politics

moral man and immoral society

Reinhold Niebuhr's *Moral Man and Immoral Society*, published in 1932, was written in his first years at Union Seminary. It was the least theological of all of his books, and among the most political. It was addressed to the global crisis of those years. In 1929, just after the beginning of Niebuhr's second academic year at Union, the Depression exposed what he soon came to describe as the economic contradictions of industrial capitalism.[1] What he had experienced in the 1920s in Detroit came crashing in on the liberal, modern world after 1929.

In 1932, the year of *Moral Man*, global crises broke what few liberal restraints remained.

In the United States, Franklin Delano Roosevelt was elected president. In Germany, however, Adolf Hitler became a German citizen in 1932, and the Nazi Party began its rise to power. Not by quirk, fascist forces rose to power in Italy and Spain. In Eastern Europe, Josef Stalin crushed resistance in the Ukraine while failing to stop famine in the USSR. In East Asia, Japan invaded China, the beginning of another war to come. Nineteen thirty-two was a year when, the world over, national and international power relations tumbled head over heels, cracking the shell of nineteenth-century modernity.

Books become classics only partly for what they say and how they say it. This is especially so for nonfiction books like *Moral Man and Immoral Society*, books whose authors think big ideas in such an uncertain time as the 1930s. If they are to endure, these books must touch something unresolved—and very possibly unresolvable—in the culture to which they were first addressed. This exactly is what Niebuhr did at the start of his first major book:

> The thesis to be elaborated in these pages is that a sharp distinction must be drawn between the moral and social behavior of individuals and of social groups, national, racial, and economic; and that this distinction justifies and necessitates political policies which a purely individualistic ethic must always find embarrassing.[2]

Individuals and groups are evidently different, but just how are groups able to be moral? The supreme triumph (if that is the word) of early-modern liberal economic thinking is in the degree to which it implanted the ludicrous idea that the individual alone—save for the invisible hand of the mysteriously abstract market—is the motor force of collective life and thus the moral source of whatever good groups may achieve.

The main, and most famous, idea of Niebuhr's *Moral Man* is that society is immoral, thus resistant to moral man's idealized ethic of love. In later years he would regret the term *immoral* as too strong. But in the 1930s it was strikingly apt to his theme. The state, and the society it means to govern, cannot escape its roots in power—in domination in particular:

> All social cooperation on a larger scale than the most intimate social group requires a measure of coercion. While no state can maintain its unity purely by coercion, neither can it preserve itself without coercion. Where the factor of mutual consent is strongly developed, and where standardized and approximately fair methods of adjudicating and resolving conflicting interests within an organized group have been established, the coercive factor in social life is frequently covert, and becomes apparent only in moments of crisis and in the group's policy toward recalcitrant individuals. Yet it is never absent.[3]

Niebuhr is here setting himself hard against both religious and secular liberalism, thus against the dominant core of American popular politics.

Niebuhr's *Moral Man* was a defense of political realism that required him to reassess two of the most troubling terms in the vocabulary of modern social and political theory—*power* and *liberalism*. They have in common a perplexing lexical vagueness. Power is what power does; but it does what it does by any means necessary—economic, social, cultural, and political. At the same time, in the modern era, power is barely discernible in the economic intimidations of the corporations, the overpowering obfuscations of the socially impressive, the disaffecting consequences of mass media, or the outright bullying of political oppressors. Yet it is there. Power does its work with money, influence, seduction, or force—or all at once; or one at one moment, another at the next.

But what did Niebuhr mean by liberalism, one of the least settled concepts in the political lexicon? Niebuhr used language carefully—a benefit of his having learned English out of the complexities of German language and thought. One supposes that over the years of his education and early professional life there were many occasions when he disciplined himself both to check the English against the German and, in the process, to think critically of American terms and the ideas they express in relation to European traditions of thought. Whatever the case, Niebuhr thought through ideas and terms with due regard for their broadest and variable meanings. His critique of liberalism in religious and secular politics would be one of the pillars of his theory of contemporary history. He understood what "liberalism"—the word and political ideal—realistically meant among its many and contradictory uses.

Originally, *liberal* had very little to do with politics. Before the nineteenth century, *liberal*, noun or adjective, meant simply "free" in several senses—freely given or generous; free from restraint; free inquiry; free speech; ample—of which the earliest usage seems to have been in respect to the free or liberal professions. As a noun used in political discriminations, *liberal* did not come into play until nineteenth-century British politics used it as a metonym for "not-conservative"—hence, the Liberals were radical Whigs opposed to the Tories, who were, and still are (though loosely), conservatives. As with all binary definitions the distinction quickly became an either/or epithet; hence John Stuart Mill (1865): "A Liberal is he who looks forward for his principles of government; a Tory looks backward."[4] Mill is credited with having given the earlier and individualistic idea of liberty a more robust political sense. Still, his views led, at their best, to the liberal suspicion of power.[5]

The classic liberalisms of Britain carried over, in modified form, to the political theories of the Jefferson, Madison, Hamilton, Adams, and others of the revolutionary generation in America—Jefferson, most famously, in the 1776 declaration of the self-evident and inalienable right to "Life, Liberty and the pursuit of Happiness." Jefferson acknowledged the British source of the American's rights, proposing

> to remind him [the British throne] that our ancestors, before their emigration to America, were the free inhabitants of the British dominions in Europe, and possessed a right which nature has given to all men, of departing from the country in which chance, not choice, has placed them, of going in quest of new habitations, and of there establishing new societies, under such laws and regulations as to them shall seem most likely to promote.[6]

It would not be until after the Civil War that the United States would seriously institutionalize state-sponsored welfare programs for widows and orphans, as well as the short-lived Freedman's Bureau for freed slaves.[7] But these measures, and those to follow, were held in check by the resistance of individualistic politics to state power.

The term *liberal* as used today in American politics is almost exclusively associated with the policies and practices for which no figure is more the embodiment than FDR in the 1930s. Roosevelt's social and economic programs to combat the Depression constituted the one briefly extended moment in American politics when a socially responsible federal government invoked its powers on the side of the poor and suffering. By contrast, in Britain left-liberal politics had its roots early in the twentieth century and came to the fore in 1922 when the Labour Party passed the Liberal Party as the leading opposition party. Thus, from time to time—the Labour Party in the United Kingdom in the 1990s, the Socialists in France in the 1980s—left parties were susceptible to classically liberal thinking in the form of experiments with market-based economic policies. These, of course, were the consequences of electoral politics following a long reign by Conservative or Gaullist regimes—attempts to adjust to a prevailing liberal (which is to say conservative) political climate. In liberal democracies, election to power usually turns on the ability of rivals to outwit opponents in the competition for votes—a market determined at the ballot less by ideology than by (mostly) economic interests. Still, ideologies and the parties that convey them make up a force in the electoral process. Thus in the United States, where no truly left or socialist party has ever been able to contest for national power, the fungibility of the liberal ideal is all the more pronounced. Walter Russell Mead has poignantly dismissed the still current, ever foolish conservative claim that liberals in America are enemies of the capitalist order. Mead defined liberalism as a "chameleon ideology"—willing, perhaps, to seek justice for the poor so long as the economic marketplace remains secure.[8]

It has proven much more difficult to formulate, and practice, a thoroughly positive idea of the American liberal. Alan Wolfe's *The Future of Liberalism*—a bold yet appreciative and persuasive study of liberalism's dilemma—sets forth seven dispositions of the liberal and speaks prominently of a liberal disposition toward "sympathy for equality." This is a small clue to the difficulties inherent in any attempt like Wolfe's to resolve the contradiction between individual rights and freedoms (Liberalism's first foundational rule) and just equalities (Liberalism's latter-day disposition).[9] Always, when (as Wolfe and most others insist) rights and freedoms come first, then justices and equalities come second—as, at best, a sympathetic attitude, not a dogged resolve. People fight for rights, not so much for sympathies. There are good reasons why free (hence: liberal) market capitalism thrives in individualistic cultures, of which the United States and the United Kingdom are primary instances.

The reality of Western history is that the modern West was built, from at least 1500 onward, in the global explorations for new wealth—for, that is, capital wealth able to expand through well-reasoned reinvestment into a continuing stream of surplus values. The ideal of progress has always been subservient to capitalism's reliance on continuous economic growth in a world where values and resources are finite. As a result, in nations like the United States, where the ideology of economic freedoms and actual market forces are the determining spheres of personal worth, ideological and practical politics are always vulnerable to the exceptions required by corporate powers. No less is liberalism, especially in the United States, a weak term precisely because it must serve to create a political exception to the power of the state.

A liberal thus was, and still is, one who is not conservative, where conservatives are taken to be those more than willing to use power (whatever that might be) to conserve their version of the truth, when their truths are nearly always the truths that redound to those who hold their privileges by tradition. Liberalism thereby stakes out the rights of the individual against those of the powerful, of which the state is the pure type and the free market the fantasy playground. "When economic power desires to be left alone," Niebuhr said of the lure of liberal individualism, "it uses the philosophy of *laissez faire* to discourage political restraint upon economic freedom."[10] Liberal individualism is the hoax that covers the reality of state interests that are bound tight to corporate greed. Liberalism is always implicated in the devious effects of power.

Liberalism and *power*—though words of quite different kinds meant to serve quite different purposes—are in effect modernity's odd couple. The one, *power*, means to account for the fact that even when there is agreement that justice is a good thing, there are always at least two opposing classes—Weber's A that wins out over B. The other, *liberalism*, means to protect A and B individuals from the rough and tumble powers of the social mechanisms of governing. In this respect, power and liberalism are concepts that, to a significant degree, are defined with each other in mind—at least in the strangely impolite quietude of modern civilization. Power, which by definition is an A property, is at best interested in protecting its A-ness. The individuals A's wish to protect are their own; B's be damned. Liberalism is the all-inclusive name for the modern need to pretend power is not what it is and that socially dominant positions are due not to coercion but to the evident brilliance, hard work, and beauty of those who attain them.

In lectures Niebuhr delivered in Rochester, New York, in 1934, just after the publication of *Moral Man and Immoral Society*, he complained that Protestantism in the United States was so dependent on modern culture that it would collapse "when the material foundations of the civilization begin to crumble."[11] Niebuhr's thinking in the early years of the 1930s was still fresh from the Detroit years and Henry Ford's vulgar capitalism that was widely offered as the sign of modernity's hope and promise. The Depression, if not by any means welcome, was at least a certification of the corruption of the modern order. Hence Niebuhr's quasi-postmodern line that the collapse of modern ideology might at least promise a more independent line of religious thought.

Whatever the influence on Niebuhr of the Social Gospel, what we see in the book of 1932 is just how far he had left its ideas behind him. In *Moral Man* he does not even mention Rauschenbusch. Instead, he is addressing himself to Marxism and Communism—what the one had promised and what the other, in Stalin, had already become. He is now set square against "liberal Christianity," of which the Social Gospel was, one might say, the best expression of an incomplete idea.

Niebuhr's early years in New York brought a significant intellectual change. They would mark the beginning of what came to be called Niebuhr's neo-orthodoxy.[12] Ironically, these were the years of his early (ultimately limited) exploration of socialism. It may seem odd that a turn to Christian orthodoxy would be associated with an interest in socialism. To be sure, the oddity is softened somewhat by recalling that these were the early years of the Great Depression, when even in the United States Roosevelt's New Deal offered at least a weak form of socialist principles. But for Niebuhr, who took a good while to warm to Roosevelt, what socialist values he had held were always framed by prior intellectual and religious commitments to his brand of biblical Protestantism. This meant a strong theory of social justice as in the Wheat and the Tares. All are in it together. None has the final word.

In the 1920s Niebuhr had been intrigued by the Social Gospel, but the attraction soon faded in the face of his deeper understanding of Henry Ford and industrial capitalism's greed. In the end, the Social Gospel remained on the near side of liberalism, with its weak theory of power and, ultimately, strong theory of individual rights. *Moral Man and Immoral Society* was the literary effect of Niebuhr's struggle in the early 1930s with the failures of liberal religion, the possibilities of socialism, and the biblical principles of social justice.

Niebuhr thought that the abiding flaw of liberal thought, including especially its religious versions, was its easy dependence on modern values. Liberal modernity trusts in prosperous markets, political goodwill, and historical progress. When it surfaces as religion, liberal culture is particularly naked and naïve. Liberal religion, especially in the 1920s, inclined toward an individual ethic of love as sufficient to an ethical critique of coercive social and economic structures. Niebuhr understood very well that a duplicitous character like Henry Ford could not possibly be "loved"—much less talked—out of his ways. Ford (and the Fordist industrial system of pure efficiency he instituted in automobile manufacturing) trusted that his ways were the wave of the future.[13]

Niebuhr, who had declared himself a tamed cynic, was certainly capable of revulsion at social and economic injustice. But his ethical objections to naïve liberalism in religion and politics went deeper by far than any social theoretical rhetoric. In a word, his realism began, as in all things, in a continuously evolving biblical theology that required a comparable realism as to the historical nature of social injustice. Liberalism inclines to define politics as the art of the possible, which, in turn, inclines toward reluctance to probe too deeply below the surfaces of social and economic appearances. Biblical religion, beginning with the Hebrew prophets, was rooted in a stern judgment on the ability of the state to do or be good, just as the gospels rebuked the wealthy and arrogant who believed they were powerful because they were good. Power, he thought, is harsh and unrelenting, but also deceptive in the promises it makes. The Gospel is not a sugar pill. It can be bitter and hard to swallow, but no more so than the brutalities of the real world. A Christian ethic can deal with a sugarcoated vulgarity only by meeting power with power.

But what exactly did Niebuhr mean by power? In the early pages of *Moral Man*, he hints at his passing flirtation with Marxism: "The disproportion of power in a complex society which began with the transmutation of the pastoral to the agrarian economy, and which destroyed the simple equalitarianism and communism of the hunting and nomadic social organization, has perpetuated social injustice in every form through all the ages."[14] One of the ways Marx's thinking bleeds through in Niebuhr's is in a romantic belief that justice is native to the more elementary social forms and, thereby, to human community. At the same time (and again like Marx) the more dominant theme already evident in *Moral Man* is of a hearty realism as to the effects of power in modern societies.

Already in 1932, Niebuhr had developed a discriminating analysis of the strengths and weaknesses of the liberal ideals in modern society:

The rise of modern democracy, beginning with the Eighteenth Century, is sometimes supposed to have substituted the consent of the governed for the power of the royal families and aristocratic classes as the cohesive force of national society. This judgment is partly true but not nearly as true as the uncritical devotees of modern democracy assume. The doctrine that government exists by the consent of the governed, and the democratic technique by which the suffrage of the government determines the policy of the state, may actually reduce the coercive factor in national life, and provide for peaceful and gradual methods of resolving conflicting social interests. But the creeds and institutions of democracy have never become fully divorced from the special interests of the commercial classes who conceived and developed them. With the increased centralisation of economic power in the period of modern industrialism, this development merely means that society as such does not control economic power as much as social well-being requires; and that the economic, rather than the political or the military, power has become the significant force of modern society. Either it defies the authority of the state or it bends the institutions of the state to its own purpose. Political power has been made responsible, but economic power has become irresponsible in modern society.[15]

Niebuhr here tenders a rudimentary but fungible theory of power in the complex industrial social forms of modern society. As coercion, power is everywhere (if not everywhere as outright coercion); at the same time it is not everywhere the same. This distinction is already a marked departure from Marx's thinking. Marx was a strict materialist in search of a new universal class able to overcome the universal evil of the capitalist class. For Niebuhr, power moves furtively according to opportunities for asserting itself—from the political to the economic sphere and, though he does not say it here, also to the cultural sphere even, perhaps especially, in the Church. It would be some time before American sociology would see these distinctions as clearly (and it is likely that Niebuhr was able to see them because of his familiarity with the writings of Max Weber, who understood modern societies in a similar way).[16]

What Niebuhr begins to achieve in *Moral Man and Immoral Society* is a realistic *and* flexible theory of power consistent with his already well-thought-through criticism of liberalism as a naïve faith in the power of the free individual to make social justice. His ideas here are incomplete in that he identified social power too much with coercion, not enough with its other less direct mechanisms, such as distortion and subjugation, which would not be seriously considered in the West until somewhat later. Yet this was 1932, when the terrible coercive force of economic greed had left millions unprotected and when, in Europe and Japan, new forms of imperial power were on the rise with comparably evil effects on the masses. The devastating effects and aftereffects of the World War of 1914 were still very much on his mind. In his 1923 fact-finding mission to Britain and Europe, Niebuhr was especially disturbed by the devastating effects of the economic retributions visited on Germany. With his own eyes he saw the poverty and hunger. The war itself had been, of course, a conflict of national forces. But the vengeance sought by the Allies in 1919 was still another, more serious, kind of political violence.

Economic misery and fascism in Europe were cut of the same soiled cloth of national immoralities: "The necessity of using force in the establishment of unity in a national community, and the inevitable selfish exploitation of the instruments of coercion by the groups that wield them, adds to the selfishness of nations. . . . When governing groups are deprived of their special economic privileges, their interests will be more nearly in harmony with the interests of the total national society."[17] Surely, lines like these, in 1932, were written with post–World War I Germany first in mind.

Niebuhr's ominous construal of state power culminates in the fourth chapter of *Moral Man*, "The Morality of Nations." This essay is nothing short of an outline of a general theory of the modern nation-state—a theory derived, once again, from his reservations about liberalism in all its forms. The nation-state had long been considered the foundational institution of liberal democracies. To the contrary, wrote Niebuhr, the liberal nation-state is based on force:

> Nations are territorial societies, the cohesive power of which is supplied by the sentiment of nationality and the authority of the state. The fact that state and nation are not synonymous and that states frequently incorporate several nationalities, indicates that the authority of government is the ultimate force of national cohesion. The fact that state and nation are roughly synonymous proves that, without the sentiment of nationality with its common language and traditions, the authority of its government is usually unable to maintain national unity.[18]

Niebuhr offers the example of the British state's long historical struggle to create and sustain national unity in Scotland and Ireland.

"The Morality of Nations" is a torrent of illustrations of the larger point. Readers today who have forgotten their world history might be put off or otherwise confused by the examples. But this is easily overcome by taking the main point. Everywhere the modern state pursued its interest, coercion followed: the United States in the Philippines, Britain in India and South Africa, Belgium in the Congo, America (again) in respect to the Caribbean and Latin America, Britain (again) in respect to the Middle East, France in North Africa, among others. Many examples, perhaps too many, make a single, devastating point:

> The morality of nations is at best mixed, at worst non-existent. Perhaps the most significant moral characteristic of the nation is its hypocrisy.

We have noted that self-deception and hypocrisy is an unvarying element in the moral life of all human beings. It is the tribute which morality pays to immorality; or rather the device by which the lesser self gains the consent of the larger self to indulge in impulses and ventures. . . . Naturally this defect in individuals becomes more apparent in the less moral life of nations. . . . Their hypocrisy is both a tribute to the growing rationality of man and a proof of the ease with which national demands may be circumvented.[19]

These were dire times. In 1932 liberal culture was failing, nowhere more than in respect to the corruption of state power. If the state is to maintain social cohesion, it has no choice but to lie—to its citizenry and to itself. Niebuhr is ferocious in his attacks on the hypocrisy of state power.

There are many aspects of Niebuhr's political thinking in this early book that would require correction in later years—and none more so that the rather tortured idea that the selfishness of nations is rooted in the inherent selfishness of individuals. The phrasing of the connection seems to contradict the book's main idea—that states are of a different, less ethical, order from individuals. Yet granting the slippage, the analogy is striking when turned on itself. Against the already narrow liberal idea that the state can do limited good, Niebuhr argues that states and the societies they aim to manage, no less than individuals, are unremittingly selfish, ruthlessly ready to pursue their interests by coercing the vulnerable. The terms are a little off, but the insistence that the national society is incapable of love, much less justice, unless it is coerced was in 1932 a powerfully original idea.

Niebuhr's *Moral Man* was a daring reconsideration of the liberal theory of rational democracy—one that avoids the materialist appeal to economic greed while also, like Marx, recognizing what the hypocritical ways of state power owe to the contradictions of its nature. The guardian of liberal national values *must* be dishonest in order to hold the nation together: "The best that can be expected of nations is that they should justify their hypocrisies by a slight measure of real international achievement, and learn how to do justice to wider interests than their own, while they pursue their own."[20] Justice is the best that can be expected of such a beast.

Yet however caught the nation is in the inevitability of its dishonesty, historically churches have hardly been less duplicitously human. Where the state coerces to cover its hypocrisies, the church is merely feeble—unable even remotely to come to terms with the injustices and failures of the immoral society. "Religion encourages love and benevolence . . . by absolutizing the moral principle of life until it achieves the purity of absolute disinterestedness and by imparting transcendent worth to the life of others."[21] One of Niebuhr's most serious doubts about organized religion—by which he meant usually, but not always, Christianity—is its inclination toward perfectionism. Whether by absolutizing moral principles or by moralizing about abstract ideals of a perfect spiritual state of being, religion tends to distract its adherents from the real political and economic concerns of this world. Thus "the full force of religious faith will never be available for the building of a just society, because its highest visions are those which proceed from the insights of a sensitive individual conscience."[22] Here he means, precisely, Protestant religion, where another sort of hypocrisy rules the roost. The individual Christian, as Luther put it best, is free to believe or not, but if he believes he is obligated to love his neighbor. Niebuhr, in his way, is just as stern in his complaint against liberal Christianity as he is against the modern nation-state.

Modern man is heir to the inherent selfishness of human nature. Preoccupied with his individuality, modern man reasserts her selfishness. No less, in modern cultures, especially in America, individualism is part and parcel of a national selfishness and a religious enthusiasm for the salvation of the individual as expressed in the so-called Great Commandment of Jesus: "Love the Lord thy God with all thy heart, and . . . thy neighbour as thyself" (Matthew 22:37, 39). As in Luther's dictum on Christian liberty, Protestant Christianity puts the emphasis on the ethic of love—and thereby exposes itself to its own and the nation's moral failure. The ethic of love may to a degree encourage justice in the nation, but insofar as it is an ethic of the individual it is perfectionistic, thus unable, even unwilling, to confront the well-structured power of the hypocritical society.

In *Moral Man and Immoral Society*, Niebuhr did not fully succeed in designing a new social or political theory, nor did he develop a systematic ethical theory. Yet there are elements of both—far more richly developed than one might expect of a still young man at the beginning of his first teaching position. He was just four years into a thirty-year tenure at Union Seminary.

Moral Man is a classic in its own right. Its genius may be that, apart from its main line of attack on liberal politics, it also serves to map the new area with which he would forever be identified. No one of his day did more to redefine and direct the field of social ethics, a topic of academic and policy studies for many. But Niebuhr's social ethics, while historically and philosophically well informed, sprang, as did much else, from his religious faith, thus from his vocation as a Protestant preacher.

Reinhold Niebuhr, the preacher without a pulpit, understood the power of the Protestant pulpit, but not simply because he was himself so powerful a platform speaker. Rather, more than for most in his line of work, Niebuhr's religious understanding of power and politics was unflinching in its attention to their significance in the secular worlds.

At the same time, he understood them because he so intently grasped the unique, if not exclusive, capacity of Protestantism to unsettle the established powers of the modern world—and nowhere more so than in the United States, the most Protestant of all modern cultures. Indeed, one of the most powerful, if treacherous, places in America is the pulpit of the Protestant churches. This because, without the regalia and atmospherics common to many other brands of religion, Protestant cults attend with ill-disguised seriousness to the weekly workplace of the preacher.

Members of any organized Protestant church may admire or loathe their preacher; but few, very few, will consider the reason a preacher's weekly declamation is a force in their lives—or, deeper still, in the history of their nation. Preaching was at the heart of Reinhold Niebuhr's work, and thus a resource to his thinking, because he had grown up with and thereafter personally experienced the hard realities a pulpit imposes on its occupant.

Preaching from pulpits runs up against fantasies that cannot be requited. The pulpit is meant to be elevated and elevating. Niebuhr's genius was that—remembering his father's life work and his own time in the Bethel Church—for more than thirty years after quitting his Detroit pulpit, he turned his academic platform into a pulpit of sorts. More important, through Niebuhr's political work and journalistic writings, he became America's most prominent postliberal intellectual by planting a pulpit in the middle of the nation's public square, thence to preach freely the word of a new global order.

The itinerant preacher and the settled pastor both preach. The prudent ones are familiar with the perils of the pulpit. Preaching can occur any which place, but when it is done week after week in a pulpit provided by a gathered congregation, it becomes an activity at once powerful and dangerous. It can be risky business to mount a pulpit, there to pronounce what words may come to mind. The preacher's risks are compounded on the side of worshipers who come expecting something. Their expectation is legitimate to the degree it is regularly disappointed.

A preacher who is also the local pastor cannot quit the village after the last handshake. He must do it all over again but days later. The word *sermon* shares a Latinate root with *semen*. Thus if the sermon is the seed of wisdom, then the pulpit is the condom meant to seal the deal. From time to time, a seed leaks through. But normally the preacher comes and does what he can, after which congregants sigh wanly, as both relax in the assurance that the deed is done for another week. Regulars to the activity well understand that as time goes by the partners may lose interest in the routine. Itinerants come and go. Pastors who are preachers remain to try to keep the dance interesting.

To understand Niebuhr one must understand the power of pulpits of all kinds. In America, political pulpits derive from the religious ones—as in England political discourse is shaped by the Oxbridge debate clubs or in France by smart-alecky retorts refined at the École Normale Supérieure. But in the United States, where the common is privileged over the elite, the pulpit is a powerful figment of public imagination. Here the pulpit is a generic platform because preaching from one is so acute to the religious habits of Protestantism, which has so influenced American moral culture.

Reinhold Niebuhr's pulpit wisdom was anything but a figment. He survived the risks of a local pulpit to invent a political one. Yet he never lost sight of the perilous power of the Protestant place from which the words are proclaimed for better or worse. To understand the Protestant effect on American politics is to understand the pulpit as a cultural institution.

In most Protestant churches, the pulpit, the physical place, is an elevated, sparsely decorated, prominently visible feature of the house of worship. By design, truly Protestant pulpits are plain, relatively barren of religious icons. The idea is that something transpires there that is meant to fashion a degree of unfettered immediacy between believers and their gods. So powerful is the effect that even the most commonplace of pulpits can conjure up a sacred aura. Among true Protestants the pulpit is special, somehow, even when worshipers cannot account for its whys and wherefores.

Other religious groups may face the sacramental table, the sacred scrolls, the holy city, or a gold-leafed Buddha, Vishnu, or Shiva to focus their religious gatherings. But Protestant congregations normally attend most directly to the pulpit from which the sacred words are passed down according to local custom. What many, even the devout, fail to recognize is the extent to which the men and women permitted week after week to mount the pulpit are just what they appear to be—men and women not remarkably distinguished by spiritual merit from those who congregate below for their weekly show. Legitimate and regular occupants of a local pulpit will from time to time rise to the standards they preach. But even the best among them is vulnerable before the bad wind that blows in the crevasse between the minister's implausibly high standing and the lowdown human interests of those in the pews.

The perils of the Protestant situation cut both ways at once; but practically speaking, the prevailing wind rises from the congregants, who, well aware of their needs, elevate their preachers to an improbable status considered necessary and sufficient unto their expectations. This is an aspect of the Protestant pulpit's power to transform a common place into a throne someone ascends under the illusion of a high calling. Other similarly adorned social positions are less opaque to the aura they bestow. Celebrities have their ways of transcending the crowds that rush to their mosh pits. They do something well enough to move their adoring fans to pay the cost of the bumps and grinds of the pit. Protestant preachers, by contrast, are judged almost exclusively on their pulpit work, which is occasionally spot on, more often sincerely undistinguished, and more times than necessary absurdly pointless. Yet people pay for it, in more ways than one.

Many preachers have had little or no training for the work. Some, like one I know of, lack any "cemetery"[23] training at all. Some interpret the sacred words more by spirit than by any reasoned appeal to evidence. "I always called you Jesus, you always called me Sonny." Some, like one television evangelist, may hide their learning behind clownish hats and eccentric ways. Even those properly trained, if there is such a thing, are trained in seminaries (not cemeteries) where the learning is usually subservient to an expectation of discernible calling and devotional habit.

Herein is the difference of the Protestant pulpit. The rabbi preaches, but a rabbi is, literally, a teacher whose learning is closely associated with her authority. A priest of any high church denomination is qualified by the authorized right to perform the sacred rites. What he may say in the pulpit thereby has little bearing on the church's reason for being. One might suppose that, like Jewish and Muslim clerics, the Protestant preacher derives legitimate authority from the office to which he has been assigned or elected. This is true; but again true with an exception. Even the strict fundamentalist, who professes the arguable meaning of the literal words of God, is little likely to interpret the sacred words strictly. No less, the evangelist who professes truth born of his experience of rebirth finds it hard sledding to press his personal Lord on others. The truth of things preached from a Protestant pulpit squares poorly with the hallowed texts because the pulpit is itself an earthbound institution lodged precariously at the upward reach of the human spirit for an unreachable mystery.

"A genuine faith," Niebuhr believed, "must recognize that it is through a glass darkly that we see; though by faith we do penetrate sufficiently to the heart of the mystery not to be overwhelmed by it."[24] This is the dilemma at the foundation of Protestantism. It is true that in many cultures, notably the American one, "protestant" ideas have spread into other major religious traditions, not to mention the culture at large. Still, there remains a distinctive quality that is more pronounced among Protestant sects. The most elemental Protestant doctrine is that no doctrine suffices—that nothing in this world ought to be taken with ultimate seriousness.[25] The Protestant truths are, by definition, beyond any religious authority—including most especially the claims of a preacher to possess a better faith.[26] In principle, all Protestants are on an equal footing as to their interpretations of the sacred texts.

No less, Protestants are prideful because, being human, they must live in despair. In this Niebuhr drew upon Søren Kierkegaard in Sickness unto Death: "Despair is the disrelationship in a relation which relates itself to itself"—which, roughly translated, means: God creates the relationship with man, then lets the created one go it on his own, to pick the forbidden fruit that upsets the applecart. Protestantism exaggerates this universal condition, in principle, by nullifying the formal rituals and doctrines that serve, falsely, to ease the despair of being left to die. In place of the Roman crucifix, which reminds the Catholic of God's sacrifice for him (and all the entailed responsibilities appertaining thereto), the Protestant churches most often display an empty cross (or nothing at all), which puts the dilemma back on the believer to trust that which is not revealed. Actual Protestant cults will fight the universal human sickness just as much as do the high churches with all their paraphernalia. But the despair reappears, most notably, in the pride and egoism that are the outward moods of the species' anxiety.

In their aggravated dread, Protestants—whether professed or simply naturalized by the culture—are like all others but for one thing. Having stood on principle by removing, or believing they had removed, the ecclesiastical assurances of relationship with their gods, their dread is more visible in their behavior. This is why excitable religious sentiment is much more common among Protestants. Niebuhr's spiritual maturity was never more on display that it was in his refusal of sentimental religious displays. He understood the full range of Protestant sensibilities but kept his own emotional counsel.

It is not that Protestants have more native human anxiety than, say, Catholics or Orthodox Jews, but that they expose themselves more to the human sickness arising from the fear of death. Their pride, also a universal human failing, may be more acute or more extreme because, Niebuhr might have said, they have fewer assurances that their faith will pay off. Still, Protestants, as a rule, are discernibly more inclined to claim a unique providence for their churches, even their nations. Seldom will those of other faiths ring the doorbell to entreat those at home to consider the state of their souls and the end of the worlds. Only a protestantized nation, like the United Sates, would so clumsily exaggerate its moral importance to universal humanity.

Yet when it comes to Protestant faith, nothing, by necessity, is ever quite what it seems or is wished for; hence the collusion between preacher and congregants. She rises to the platform to do her best to meet the expectation of special wisdom; they keep quiet below in the hope that the one above will achieve what she cannot and, according to the rules, must not. There are no winners in this game—save when preacher and congregants strike a happy enough human accord that allows them to conspire in breaching the rules that make their brand of religion special to them.

As in all well-intended masquerades, the participants are not long at ease with the trickery involved. This is what makes the pulpit at once powerful and dangerous. The power issues from the effort required on both sides of the pulpit to keep the thing working as well as it can. The danger thereby is inherent in the instability of the relationship—an instability that Niebuhr respected as the central dilemma of human life: "It is not easy to preserve a decent balance between the ethical urge to realize perfection in history and the religious need of reconciliation with imperfection."[27] We want more than can be had—a ubiquitous quandary that binds more tightly in the Protestant churches.

One wants to preach well, or to trust the preacher honestly, even when one knows in one's heart of hearts that something is not quite right. Sooner or later the truth outs, though seldom in so many words. At that moment one or another of the minister's human failings is seized upon as the occasion to break the code of silence. More often than not, the complaints pass through the local body of Christ like canned meat through a dog. The better churches learn to live with the mess, even to respect it. The average ones will kill the dog. Among Protestants there is no available arbiter of the circumstance, where other religious groupings have bishops or mullahs who can cut the dog from the flock or condemn the offending sheep to slaughter.

These are the human elements in the spiritual dilemmas created in and around the Protestant pulpit, of which Niebuhr was acutely sensible: "If the strong sense of frustration which comes over me so frequently on Sunday Evening and to which many other parsons have professed is merely due to physical lassitude or whether it arises from the fact that every preacher is trying to a bigger thing than he is equal to—and fails. I have an uneasy feeling that it may be native honesty of the soul asserting itself."[28] If the essential Protestant principle requires acceptance of the limits to human understanding of divine things, then the Protestant pulpit is situated at the crosshairs of two finely drawn but definite vectors of power. From the one descends the sacred truths that are preposterously unavailable to authoritative definition, yet imperative to the conduct of the religious life. From the other rises the thirst of men and women to hear if not *the* Word, *some* words that will comfort or inspire as need or taste dictates. One hesitates to stipulate that the former vector is vertical and the latter horizontal because the Protestant notion is that God is at once absent from history *and* totally present in it.

This is the protestantizing paradox which is nowhere better expressed than in Martin Luther's *Treatise on Christian Liberty* (1520): "A Christian man is the most free lord of all, and subject to none; a Christian man is the most dutiful servant of all, and subject to every one." The Protestant revolt began in a declaration of religious liberty that put the responsibility on the individual conscience if not exactly to represent God's presence in history, to act as though one's actions were the earthly sign of his absence.

Niebuhr obviously agreed with Luther's emphasis on the paradox of faith—but not without identifying its paralyzing effects.[29] The Christian is free, yes, but at the same time indentured. The moral obligations of this paradox can freeze the believer in his tracks, as over the centuries it has Lutherans who are inclined to retreat into the Church to let the world have its way. Still, Niebuhr understood well that Luther's paradoxical idea of Christian liberty was in the tradition of Protestant spiritual paradox from Paul to Augustine to Kierkegaard, which led to modern individualism.

Individual freedoms are not easily reconciled with the demands of social order, because the free individual and restricting society power press unevenly against each other. This is the dilemma at the moral foundations of modern life, which, in turn, is one step removed from modernity's political and moral paradox: How are individual rights to be squared with social justice?

In its own way, Niebuhr's political thinking took up the problem of power and its disorienting effects as simultaneously also a question of both the sacred and profane aspects of human experience. It may not at first be apparent, but the complicating element in real politics, whether religious or secular, is always power. When power is real, it redounds, with rare exception, to the benefit of those who possess it.

Niebuhr first encountered raw and abusive secular power in Detroit. In retrospect it is more common today to think of large corporate bosses as ruthless and greedy. To be fair, Niebuhr was not among the first generation of social critics to expose the social evils of capitalist powers. That distinction goes back at least to Marx and Engels's first systematic criticisms of capitalist exploitation of the worker in the 1840s. Then, of course, the familiar characterization of the superrich of the last decades of the nineteenth century as robber barons was an illocutionary thrust of a popular discontent with the worker's suffering in the new industrial age. Still, what set Niebuhr apart was that in the years before the market collapse of 1929, he began a unique journey toward a critique of social and economic power in the industrial age that, in due course, was neither Marxist or liberal—neither in tone or substance, even though he borrowed key ideas from both and from other traditions of social thought. This required his working through the well-meaning but inherently inadequate ideology of the liberal-left Social Gospel, an ideology that directed political action against overriding social forces of the modern era but still assigned moral agency to the pure-hearted Christian individual. By contrast, Marxism in most if not all of its variants took what might appear (and has appeared) to many to be an opposite approach—that of beginning with the diagnosis of the inherent evil of structural capitalism as the source of the individual's moral and human alienation from himself and his fellows. Marx, at least the Marx of the major theoretical writings from the 1840s to the 1860s, assigned the moral prospect of change to an inherent contradiction of the economic system. Hence the famous line at the end of the *Manifesto* in 1848—"Workers of the world unite; you have nothing to lose but your chains." At first blush, the line presents as a call to working-class revolution when in fact it is a description of the condition that might make revolution *possible*. This is the major chord that comes to the fore twenty years later in the brilliant political implications of the structural contradiction of capitalism—that the bourgeoisie *must* pursue profit even to the point of destroying its own system by pushing the human to the limits of her endurance.

Yet between liberal theories of power as moral agency and socialism's doctrines of power as the evil of the dominant class, Niebuhr recognized that it was not possible to distinguish the individual as the source of good from the social as the object of reform, or even revolution. Hence, *Moral Man and Immoral Society*, where *man* is effectively the individual and *society* the social force. Neither one nor the other can enjoy privilege of priority in the order of social things. What Niebuhr began, at least, to see in the later years in Detroit in the 1920s is that the Roaring Twenties in America blew an ill wind for the working poor.

The underlying dilemma of liberal politics is that it trusts too much—trusts that it knows what is to be known, believes its values are essentially good, hence capable of changing the world, thus trusts that it can do what needs to be done. Conservative politics, however corrupt or unscrupulous it can be, is truly without scruples of the liberal kind. As Bill Clinton often said of his conservative opponents: They believe in their ideologies, the facts be damned.[30] When digging a hole, if they do not find a fact, they keep on digging. We liberals, he went on, believe in facts; when digging for facts, if we don't find them, we dig another hole. Would that this were true. Liberals may in truth have better facts, but over time they seldom win against conservatives because they are innocent about power. FDR, JFK, LBJ, and Clinton won, when they did, because they were liberals who also used power firmly—which often means abandoning fact and value for the fight.

This, however, was not the realism Niebuhr espoused. His politics were fact based, and certainly informed by values of a specific kind. But he meant to straddle the fine line between the hard nose and soft heart, between the facts and the ideology, or—as Christians often put it—between the world and the Church.

In his attempt to work out a Christian realism, Detroit was just the beginning. The hard facts of industrial manufacturing's ignorance of, perhaps refusal to seek, economic justice for workers were sharpened by his faith, which then was still deeply influenced by the more innocent liberal values of the Social Gospel. In those years facts seem to have eroded faith in the Social Gospel.

It would not be until the 1930s and 1940s in New York City that the fully material postliberal left realism would emerge— this, in part, because of the changing facts of modern America. Remember that Niebuhr believed, rightly I think, that the United States did not truly leave its nineteenth century behind until 1929, the year of the market collapse and the year after he began his career in New York City. Thus the chastening effect of the global Depression: to bring home to America what the rest of the world already realized after 1914—that the naïvetés of nineteenth-century liberalism were limited at best, perhaps futile in the world as it had come to be. For Niebuhr, Ford's merciless conniving was one thing; a global crisis in capitalism another. Whatever remained of his faith in Social Gospel–type liberalism, its influence had waned to almost nothing. This is the lesson of *Moral Man and Immoral Society.* What remained was for him to work through to another more demanding ethical theory that could inform what one was to do in the face of economic crises, world wars, fascism, communism, and all the rest that characterized the 1930s and 1940s in America and the world.

That working through would come to fruition in and about 1940. The economic collapse was, of course, important in the sense that especially for Niebuhr its evidence put liberal religion in an entirely different light—and not a bright one. Henry Ford's greed was small by contrast to the global collapse of capital markets. Nineteen twenty-nine exposed the world system itself as at least vulnerable and at worst corrupt beyond words. Ninety years later, the crash of 2009 would arouse the ghosts of capitalism's false promises.

Yet the 1930s were all the more salient for Niebuhr because of his personal roots in Germany and German culture. Fascism in his virtual homeland and in Europe at large demanded of him a wholesale reconsideration of his thinking on politics and human nature—a rethinking that would be evident in his masterwork of the early 1940s, *The Nature and Destiny of Man*. Niebuhr's rethinking would be all the more severe and wrenching in proportion to the enormity of the global events with which he attempted to come to terms. For one thing, the rethinking required a realism in practice, as distinct from a realist philosophical critique of the prevailing ideas, such as those of the Social Gospel. The challenge was then, as in the 1840s, to change the world, not just to think it.

Real events demand real politics. But here another aspect of the situation Niebuhr faced in 1940 came into play. Political realism when practiced by those *not* in state or corporate power can and should be quite a different matter from a realism of the powerful—the class of those, more broadly, in political, economic, and cultural power. Machiavelli was advising princes—the powerful. A realism for political work from a position out of power is a very different matter and one that was implicitly acknowledged in Niebuhr's *Moral Man and Immoral Society*, where society is crippled with respect to justice because it works on the realist principle of pursuing its own interests. By contrast, the individual can do little more than love—and love locally—when it comes to changing state and other large social powers. But in the then-reigning religious culture, love is a virtue that is powerless before collective interests.

Thus for Niebuhr the challenge in 1940 was how to define and act upon a political realism that refused to devolve into a pietism of the good man, thus to shrink before the powers of the state and society. To be sure, he had worked the means of resisting state power—voluntary associations like the churches, unions, social action groups, organizations of various kinds devoted to social change.

But in 1940 he took a step that had long been in the offing—that of personally organizing a political group meant to have the effect, if not the form, of a political party. By 1940 Niebuhr had overcome his socialist instincts while clinging to his resistance to FDR. Still, he was not ready to devote himself permanently and fully to, say, the Democratic Party, which, especially then, was largely controlled by Dixiecrats from the deep and racist South, as the Republican Party was already controlled by corporate business interests.

Niebuhr's third-force political organization was the Union for Democratic Action, the UDA, which he brought into being and urged along by his uniquely "charismatic force."[31] It was but one of many politically interested organizations of which he was a leader—prominent among them was the American Friends of German Freedom, as well as his magazine *Christianity and Crisis.*[32] From the founding of the UDA, as well as other of his involvements, the years on either side of 1940 were a cascade of global political concerns—the plight of Jewish people in Europe, the necessity of establishing a state for international Jewry, the rejection of pacifism and the obligation to engage political evil in war, and, after the war, the liberal opposition to communism. The UDA eventually fell away in favor of the Americans for Democratic Action (ADA), which in 1947 Niebuhr cofounded with Arthur Schlesinger, Jr., Eleanor Roosevelt, John Kenneth Galbraith, and Walter Reuther—the top echelon of left-liberal notables in the United States. Through the 1960s the ADA was, if not quite a formal party organization, a highly influential group; it continues today to be an effective proponent of globally engaged political action.

For other left-wing people the ADA's most notorious stance was its fervent anticommunism, which Niebuhr shared. Those not acquainted with the subtlety of his political philosophy tend to be suspicious of Niebuhr's core ideology. Naturally, there were others who (if quietly) did not approve of his work on behalf of Jews and eventually of the founding of Israel. Even more, on the Left, there was a hostility to his rejection of pacifism and his anticommunism. Still today, these internal disputes are weaknesses of the American Left. As opposed to the Right, the Left is more inclined to eat its own—often in the name of a principle of virtuous progressive commitments or under a presumption that it has the upper hand when it comes to political righteousness and facts. Niebuhr himself lost (or gave up) a good many friendships from his earlier days. This is the one period, until he was crippled by stroke in 1952, during which he became more combative in pursuit of his ethical and political values.

For Niebuhr, well-informed deep thought tested by hard political work could (and did) lead to a still deeper, enduring understanding of human nature and the struggle for justice. Soon, even *Moral Man and Immoral Society*'s sharp rejection of mere individualism would fade to the background of a vastly more complex, if impossibly challenging, political ethic of which the foundational principle remained true to his rethinking in the 1930s and 1940s:

The weak are not without their power. The power of the weak, when it rises above collusion with the strong, is the power to resist the powerful. The weak, being greater in number, by definition, have less at stake in the established order that privileges the rights of the strong. As a result, when conditions are right, should the weak be moved to join hands, their resistance can disrupt, occasionally crush, the arrangements that made them weak. Then, however, they must themselves assume power, hence the political upper hand; either that or they must cede the power to some others. Either way, history has not been kind to the prospect of the once-weak who take power. Like those they overthrew, the newly powerful fail (as a rule) to form new social orders enduringly able to correct the social injustices they sought to overcome in the first place. There are no easy answers, Niebuhr concluded, either to politics or to faith.

It is often said, and not without good reason, that the American Revolution is the one clear case where revolution led to a better social arrangement. Niebuhr was a stern critique of American culture and politics who also appreciated America's foundational values as superior to other democracies:

> In our own country . . . realism was introduced particularly by the author of the Constitution, James Madison. Without this realism the democracy of France soon degenerated into Jacobin fanaticism and ultimately to Bonapartist absolutism.[33]

In the early years of the republic—from 1789 to 1825 or so—this was largely, if not completely, true. But in the long run the good of the American ideal reverted to liberal form. Passion for individual rights overwhelmed commitment to social justices, as in liberal cultures they generally do. In liberal political cultures, as in the modern era since 1848, freedoms have been market freedoms—the core doctrine of industrial and postindustrial capitalism. When markets are meant to be free, then rights have tended to be the rights necessary for capitalism to thrive—rights to private property, freedoms from state regulations, rights to free labor (which turn out to be rights of the powerful to control wages and suppress unions), freedoms from taxation, and the like.

Liberal democracies like the United States believe free markets are effective, for which conviction they stipulate, without persuasive evidence, that individuals are somehow or other of a higher order from complexly structured social institutions. Hence liberal democracies are caught on the horns of a dilemma of their own making by focusing on rights as if justices were a lesser matter. In no other era but the modern has this dilemma been more acute for the least powerful and less well resolved in favor of social fairness. Power thus is always at the nub of the modern dilemma, which expresses itself one way in secular (or allegedly secular) politics and another in religious (and particularly Christian) thinking. Niebuhr came to the settled opinion that realism in ethics and politics amounted to an honest suspicion in respect to power: "Realism has the merit of describing the power realities which underlie all large scale social integrations whether in Egypt, Babylon or Rome where a dominant city-state furnished the organizing power for the Empire. It also describes the power realities of national states, even democratic ones, in which a group, holding the dominant form of social power, achieves oligarchic rule, no matter how much modern democracy may bring such power under social control."[34] In fact, the problem may be *more* troubling in religious philosophies, if only because, in their pure forms, religious institutions tend to retreat before the powers of this world.

In a reflection on the hazards of the ministry at a conference at Union in 1953, Niebuhr made a more refined assessment of the problem than any found in *Leaves from a Notebook*. On the one hand, he said: "From the standpoint of the gospel, we must regard power, or the wisdom or the security of any man, as not being as significant as he tries to make himself believe that it is." At the same time: "If you do not relate this faith to the structures of the world, . . . the Christian faith may degenerate into obscurantism."[35] Power believes in itself. However much faith would wish otherwise, it must deal with the reality of worldly powers. Otherworldly religions tend to play down the politics of social differences in this life, which are, in effect, the politics of the rights of the powerful over the social and economic needs of the weak. Render unto Caesar yes; but unto the gods, what? Yet in the end, in thoroughly Protestant gatherings, everyone is more or less free to make up her own mind, even if at some peril to her soul. Individuals are perfectly free to come and go as they please.

This is what makes the Protestant *churches* (as distinct from their religious ideologies) so appealing in cultures where free thought is a prominent secular value. It is devilishly hard for Protestants to examine the actual beliefs of candidates for inclusion. Individuals aspiring to membership may be required to witness to their conversion, to recite a creed, to perform various acts of contrition. But these are tepid by contrast to churches where, by canonical rule, the examination can be failed. The Protestant always has recourse to the Protestant principle. No earthly authority has the right to stand between God and believer—though among the pious there are always those, being human, who will give it a shot. The Christian individual's conscience has the final word in this world.

The genius of the Protestant principle is that it is also a reality principle, as Niebuhr's friend and colleague Paul Tillich put it:

The Protestant principle, the source and judge of Protestantism, is not to be confused with the "Absolute" of German idealism or with the "Being" of ancient and recent philosophy. It is not the highest ontological concept derived from an analysis of the whole of being; it is the theological expression of the true relation between the unconditional and the conditioned or, religiously speaking, between God and man. As such, it is concerned with what theology calls "faith," namely, the state of mind in which we are grasped by the power of something unconditional which manifests itself to us as the ground and judge of our existence. *The power grasping us in the state of faith is not a being beside others, not even the highest; it is not an object among objects, not even the greatest; but it is a quality of all beings and objects, the quality of pointing beyond themselves and their finite existence to the infinite, inexhaustible, and unapproachable depth of their being and meaning.* The Protestant principle is the expression of this relationship. It is the guardian against the attempts of the finite and conditioned to usurp the place of the unconditional in thinking and acting. It is the prophetic judgment against religious pride, ecclesiastical arrogance, and secular self-sufficiency and their destructive consequences.[36]

Though Tillich's basic philosophy was very different from Niebuhr's, on this they shared a considerable agreement. In the end, Tillich is more severe in his judgment on the reality of Protestant church behavior: "It is the historical fate of Protestantism that it has been driven in a direction which, although understandable in the frame of world history, does not express the possibilities of the Protestant principle and may prove ultimately disastrous."[37] Niebuhr could be just as biting in his judgment of the historical reality of Protestantism. Yet perhaps because unlike Tillich he had not experienced firsthand the collapse of the German churches before the Nazis, Niebuhr tended to emphasize the promises of biblical religion: "The Christian faith is the right expression of the greatness and weakness of man in relation to the mystery and meaning of life."[38] Either way, the fundamental weakness of all actual religious institutions is that they seldom attain the grandeur of their principles.

The burden added among serious Protestants is that whether or not they understand the theology of the Protestant principle, sooner or later it catches up with them. Either the realities of power or the paradox of their faith in a conscience that cannot know the object of that faith will rise up to hit the sober Protestant in the gut. Niebuhr's first truly great book addressed the moral contradictions between faith and power.

Social ethics is not to be confused with philosophical ethics, on the one hand, or social sciences, on the other. It is neither a formal study of the truth of moral life nor an empirical science. Philosophical ethics serves to derive or imagine an ethical *Ought*—that is, a strong principle of the good to which the group ought to aspire. The social and political sciences, by contrast, mean to study the *Is* of social things—that is, the empirical realities of a social order.

Social ethics, then, is neither one nor the other, even though it draws on both philosophy and the social sciences and more, most especially history. Social ethics, in effect, is the work of applying a well-thought-through *Ought* to a realistic *Is* in order to answer the question, *What is to be done?* Action without values is mindless. Values without realism are absolutistic theories uninterested in effective action. Niebuhr lived by action when he was not disabled. His social ethics were theories oriented to practices informed by an original Christian social ethic.

Niebuhr's next step as a scholar is evident already in the 1935 book *An Interpretation of Christian Ethics*—clearly the result of his first years of scholarship and teaching in Christian social ethics at Union Seminary. As *Moral Man* had been essentially a social theory that criticized the political naïveté of Christian ethics in liberal cultures, *Interpretation* was the spelling out of the theological details of his ethical theory. Yet even in this more traditionally theological book, Niebuhr's target is the failure of liberal culture to take a historically realistic attitude toward human suffering. The first lines of the introduction could not be clearer:

Protestant Christianity in America is, unfortunately, unduly dependent upon the very culture of modernity, the disintegration of which would offer a more independent religion a unique opportunity. Confused and tormented by cataclysmic events in contemporary history, the "modern mind" faces the disintegration of its civilization in alternate moods of fear and hope, of faith and despair. The culture of modernity was the artifact of modern civilization, product of its unique and characteristic conditions, and it is therefore not surprising that its minarets of the spirit should fall when the material foundations of the civilization begin to crumble.[39]

This was 1935. The catastrophic First World War had ruined the hope of Europe. Hitler was already in power. The Great Depression still crippled the global economy, with no relief in sight. Liberal trust in love and progress was in ruins. What would come after the Second World War was a kind of liberal restoration, but even then the earlier innocence of trust in free markets and moral individuals would be diminished, never the same as before.

Moral Man and Immoral Society, unlike *Leaves from the Notebook of a Tamed Cynic*, was not even remotely a book about preaching. Still, while the duplicitous powers of the pulpit do not explicitly figure in this book, the pulpit lurks below surface presentations in the power of religion in American political life.

Like religions of all kinds, liberal governments must struggle with the contradiction between professed values and real practices. The United States Constitution prohibits an official state religion. Yet the airwaves are choked by unembarrassed evocations of God as the guarantor of American providence. Once again, though in a different sense, a pulpit looms in the breach between the ideal and the real. In the civic order the pulpit in question is less part of the furniture of local churches than a generalized platform of the social imagination. A people like the Americans who think of their nation as divinely ordained and of themselves as the planet's hardest-working and, in some ill-defined way, "best" people will be willing—indeed, more than willing—to enter into the illicit contract the pulpit requires. In a local church, congregants will feel but ignore the incongruities the pulpit creates. So, too, in the social sphere, the citizenry will cast their eyes away from atrocities committed in the name of the people. In both, the preacher must be caught with his pants down for the crisis to spill out.

Are Americans the only people trapped in this dilemma? Certainly not, if Niebuhr is right about the hypocrisies required for a nation to manage itself: "If social cohesion is impossible without coercion, and coercion impossible without the creation of social injustice, and the destruction of injustice is impossible without the use of further coercion, are we not in an endless cycle of social conflict?"[40] The principal difference in America is that the endless cycle of conflict and disavowal is more intense. This because, for the historical time being, only in America are the moral stakes so high. A nation that has come to think of itself as history's most moral people will overcome the contradiction inherent to the proposition by defining its ethics as a morality of intentions. If we *intend* our actions to be good, thus shall they be. Adjust the means to the end. Where the goal is to be the best, then the sufficient means are the motives. People who think of themselves as good have only to be sincere in their thinking. They are, hence, native utilitarians.

This is not to say that Niebuhr thought of Americans as any more dastardly than other peoples. America, in fact, was to him among the more creative of modern democracies. America was, if anything, an irony—economically powerful, culturally innocent. "We have thus far sought," he would say some twenty years later in the affluent 1950s, "to solve all our problems by the expansion of our economy [which] cannot go on forever and ultimately we must face some vexatious issues of social justice."[41] Such is the way the American civil religion exaggerates its exception to the dishonesty of all modern nations.

Moral Man was hardly a perfect book. As the years went by Niebuhr would correct some of its flaws, or at least regret them. He would not have given the moral individual so much credit, nor would he have implied that society was *simply* immoral. Still, the problem retrospectively thrust on him was that in 1932 the book was so ahead of its time that later readers might expect more than perhaps could be reasonably expected. If power is effectively the intruder upon the uneven relation between individuals and societies, then, at least, the deficiencies of Niebuhr's theory of power beg for comment.

In particular, and again, two aspects of power that Niebuhr did *not* understand are together contributions to a theory of the ways power works to coerce *gently*, even unconsciously. One is by systematic *distortion* of the society's cultural apparatus, as it has been called. The other is by a process of *subjugation*, in the sense of a process whereby the society actively creates its individuals as subjects who will give it their allegiance. *Coercion* is external and, so to speak, from the top down—dominants acting openly on subordinates. *Distortion* is internal though still from the dominant class on the masses. *Subjugation* is both internal and, oddly, from the bottom up—subordinates living by the dominant creed.[42]

Coercion, by contrast, may justify itself in rhetoric, but it does its nasty work in the economic and political spheres. The pure form of the theory of coercive power is, of course, Marxism with its leading idea that society is simply materialistic greed and that the dominant bourgeois class works actively to oppress the workers by any efficient means necessary. Though Marx had an elemental theory of the inversion of cultural powers that could be liberated in the revolution, his leading theme was that culture in general and religion in particular are opiates pushed by the capital class to drug the masses. Though Niebuhr was critical of Marx and Marxism, he did not see clearly that coercion is only part of the story of power's way of working.[43]

Niebuhr the preacher might have been the one, in an earlier time, to have diagnosed not just the hazards attached to a pulpit but the way the pulpit, in both the religious and civic senses, is a medium of power that often works to distort a culture and subjugate a people.

Still, Niebuhr can be readily excused for not having appreciated the indirect and internal ways that power works on individuals. For one thing, in *Moral Man and Immoral Society*, he was still in the process of settling accounts with the Social Gospel and Marxism. He had already arrived at one of his more devastating criticisms of the Marxist scheme—that it was no less perfectionist than liberalism—by which he included the whole of liberal culture. Marx's notion that the short-run coercive aspects of the revolution against the bourgeois class would eventually fade away in the coming classless society was naïve in the first place and, already by 1932, well refuted by evidence of the evils perpetrated by Stalin.

Also, though in Germany the prescient social theorists of the Frankfurt School were beginning to develop the distortion theory of power, there is no reason to suppose that in 1932 Niebuhr would have been familiar with those still undeveloped ideas. Theodor Adorno and Max Horkheimer were just beginning and, like others critical of the civic status quo, they were vulnerable before the rising tide of fascism. Yet as the 1930s wore on, in more ways than one, it became clear that the Nazis, though a brutal coercive force, also had set about to propagandize in public and private ways. Hitler was nothing if not a master of public rhetoric. In time it became clear that the Nazis had also set about to rewrite the terms of the culture—even the dictionaries of the German language—to subject schoolchildren to a distorted culture (as in "*hate*, an attitude properly directed at Jews"). Much of this specific history of the distortion of cultures did not come to general knowledge until well after World War II. It would be still another quarter-century before Michel Foucault in France would fully develop the subjugation theory of power. So Niebuhr could not be held to account for a failure to see aspects of power that no one else had seen.

Moral Man and Immoral Society was a work of genius that rocked the foundations of left and liberal thinking in Niebuhr's time. Today it comes down as a political and social theory that offers a way around the crippling effects of decades of Cold War ideology that linger still in the fundamentally silly idea that socialist values and programs are of a different order from liberal (which is to say, conservative) ideologies. Niebuhr took on this problem in *Moral Man*, which, as we shall see, allowed this one book to enjoy its most enduring influence on American politics in the second half of the twentieth century, which in turn establishes its value for the first half of the twenty-first.

After *Moral Man and Immoral Society*'s most important essay, "The Morality of Nations," there follow four chapters (5 through 8) that are, essentially, a systematic evaluation of the extent to which socialism fully participates in the futility of liberal politics: "The Ethical Attitudes of the Privileged Class" (they are the source and cause of hypocrisy in politics); "Ethical Attitudes of the Proletarian Class" (they have a just grievance but, especially in the United States, they will not act to effect change); "Justice Through Revolution" (way too violent); "Justice Through Political Force" (way too much like naïve liberal faith). As earlier he had clarified his criticisms of liberal politics, here he links liberal thought to socialism in ways that then were surprising to those still infatuated with Marxism. Though each of these four chapters presents itself as political theory, they are collectively a clearing of the decks for *Moral Man*'s second most important essay, "The Preservation of Moral Values in Politics" (chapter 9). Here Niebuhr's applied social ethic begins to emerge; and here we encounter what may well be the single most influential of his essays on the course of American political history. Its effect would not come into play for another thirty years.

It is well known that the Reverend Martin Luther King, Jr., considered Niebuhr one of the most important influences on his political thinking. Niebuhr's chapter on moral values in politics was the single most important resource for King's nonviolent political tactics. King refers repeatedly, in writings and speeches, to *Moral Man and Immoral Society* and to Niebuhr's ideas. "My reading of the works of Reinhold Niebuhr," he said, "made me aware of the complexity of human motives and the reality of sin at every level of man's existence."[44] King's biographer Taylor Branch argues that his nonviolent tactics were influenced far more by Niebuhr than by the other oft-cited source: "He almost never spoke of Gandhi personally and his comments about Gandhism were never different than his thoughts about nonviolence in general. By contrast, he invoked Niebuhr in every one of his major books, always with a sketch of *Moral Man and Immoral Society*. He confessed that he was 'enamored' of Niebuhr, who 'left me in a state of confusion.' "[45] The confusion, it seems, had a maturing effect on King.

King had read Niebuhr's book in 1950 during his last year at Crozer Theological Seminary in Philadelphia. King was at a crossroads. His overbearing father, Martin Sr., had expected him to return to his Ebenezer Baptist Church in Atlanta, eventually to take up the church's ministry and to continue the high bourgeois life he had made for the King family. From all outward appearances Martin Jr. was suited to the expectation. He was a bit of a dandy in school. He had gone to Morehouse, the famously elite black bourgeois college in Atlanta. His father's wealth, from business as well as church work, provided fine clothes, comfortable living, social standing, and new cars. The son enjoyed billiards, smoking, fancy talk, girls—habits that continued for a while longer through seminary and graduate school (and at least one that remained a lifelong habit).

In fact, King's uncommon gifts as a public speaker were not so much an inheritance as a trained art. In seminary, fellow students would crowd the classrooms and chapel whenever King preached. But according to Branch, his rhetorical skills were at least in part derived from the vanity within and the pressures without for him—like all black preachers in the bourgeois churches in that day—to stand above others in order to become the local race man. In seminary King would, literally, play word games with himself and others at school—learning new multisyllabic words, practicing rhythmic delivery. In his youth he was like other bourgeois youth—a bit of a show-off. Though King lacked W. E. B. Du Bois's remarkable intelligence, he possessed the charm Du Bois lacked. Both qualities were prime instances of the social vanities of educated black men in an earlier day.

Moral Man and Immoral Society fixed King's course on graduate studies. He probably wanted to put some more distance between himself and his father's plans for him. He surely hungered for the prestige of a graduate degree. But if Branch is correct, the confusion aroused by his reading of Niebuhr also pushed him to think and study more deeply. Martin's studies at Boston University did not cure him of his bourgeois pretenses, but those additional years apart fortified his wish to set out on his own and to seek challenges his father could not have appreciated.

In 1954, four years after reading Niebuhr at Crozer, King became pastor of the Dexter Avenue Baptist Church in Montgomery, Alabama. The decision to accept this call instead of returning to Atlanta disappointed his father. Daddy King, however, would soon have much more to worry about. On December 5, 1955, a year after arriving in Montgomery, Martin Luther King, Jr., was chosen to lead the Montgomery Improvement Association—the movement begun by the inspiring action of Rosa Parks. He would not be twenty-seven for another month. He immediately became a national and international figure of an influence unimaginable but a few months before. The ascent put him in unthinkable danger.

If anyone in American history knew how to work the pulpit, it was King. And the pulpit he worked was less that of a given church than that of the nation as a whole. King's nonviolent methods would be attacked soon enough as too liberal, too integrationist, too naïve about white hypocrisy. But this criticism betrayed a superficial understanding of his use of nonviolent force to change the ways of the American South and the laws of the United States.

Certainly King was thoroughly familiar with the ideas and actions of Mohandas Gandhi in South Africa and India from the 1890s to the 1940s. But King's familiarity came primarily, it seems, from reading Niebuhr's book, especially "Preservation of Moral Values in Politics," which was the beginning, if not the completion, of Niebuhr's social ethic. At the end of *Moral Man*, Niebuhr, having argued the inadequacy of the liberal Social Gospel and all other forms of liberal politics, and having demonstrated the limits of Marxism, was left with the key question a social ethic must answer. If the *Ought* is justice, and the *Is* favors a feeble individualist ethic overwhelmed by the coercive state, then *What is to be done?* The answer Niebuhr provided would change King and the nation.

Niebuhr had already dismissed revolutionary violence, while considering forms of political force that would coerce the social whole toward justice even at the risk of unintended violence. He was referring to the strike, the boycott, and civil disobedience— all of which can obviously cause suffering for others (deprivation of vital services, loss of jobs and income, bloodshed). Niebuhr clearly had in mind Gandhi's nonviolent movement in India (in which many were killed) when he pointed out "one of the great triumphs of his method," namely:

> One of the most important results of a spiritual discipline against resentment in a social dispute is that it leads to an effort to discriminate between the evils of a social system and situation and the individuals who are involved in it. Individuals are never as immoral as the social situations in which they are involved and which they symbolize.[46]

In 1957, twenty-five years after Niebuhr wrote these words, King, having won the long day in Montgomery, reflected on the lessons he had learned in the yearlong bus boycott:

> We had to get over the fact that the nonviolent resister does not seek to humiliate or defeat the opponent but to win his friendship and understanding. . . . The end of violence or the aftermath of violence is bitterness. The aftermath of nonviolence is reconciliation and the creation of a beloved community. A boycott is never an end within

itself. It is merely a means to awaken the sense of shame within the oppressor but the end is reconciliation, the end is redemption. . . . *We had to make it clear also that nonviolent resistance seeks to attack the evil system rather than individuals who happen to be caught in the system.*[47]

King's words could well have been taken directly from Niebuhr.

To be sure, Gandhi's example and his ideal of *Satyagraha* (soul-force) were elemental to Niebuhr's thinking and thus to King's.[48] To suggest that Niebuhr was the decisive influence on King's political thinking is not to say Gandhi was not, for King and others, the originator and exemplar of the nonviolent strategy. What Niebuhr added (and may have been able to add because he was dealing with states, not colonial administrators) was a theory of state power that used hypocrisy to mask its brutalities. Niebuhr's politics were, in effect, an implicit theory of social structures in which power must always be understood as working in various ways up and down the structured system that includes the state and its apparatuses as well as the corporate interests and the agencies and groups dependent on them.

Gandhi's Satyagraha was, like many elements of Niebuhr's political theory, first and foremost a religious, or spiritual, doctrine. Insofar as it became a political method, it might have been more a tactic than a strategy. Gandhi, a lawyer trained in London, certainly understood the structure of the British Empire, but Gandhi's principle of soul-force was applied in Africa and India against overwhelming colonial forces and from outside the structures of power. In the confrontations, Gandhi's focus was on the face of the other:

I will give you a talisman. Whenever you are in doubt, or when the self becomes too much with you, apply the following test. Recall the face of the poorest and the weakest man [woman] whom you may have seen, and ask yourself, if the step you contemplate is going to be of any use to him [her]. Will he [she] gain anything by it? Will it restore him [her] to a control over his [her] own life and destiny? In other words, will it lead to swaraj [freedom] for the hungry and spiritually starving millions? Then you will find your doubts and your self melt away.[49]

Beginning with the Montgomery movement, 1955–56, King's focus in the struggle was on the structured evil that could be seen *in the face of the other*. To put the immorality of states and their structures first is to work from within a long-term strategy. The sheriffs with their hoses and dogs stood before him as tragic instances of the immoral system, representatives of years of racial injustice that had been ingrained in the nation's economy and culture.

To begin, as King did, with the structured system is to begin as Niebuhr's social ethic required—a strategy for ethical action that takes equal account of the spiritual values required and of the structured realities of the situation. The movement's victory in Montgomery in 1955–56 did not immediately lead to reconciliation between the races. A decade later a younger generation of black revolutionaries would abandon the integrationist goals of the early civil rights movement in the United States; still: "The arc of the moral universe is long, but it bends toward justice." Niebuhr's influence added to King's rhetoric the touch of realism that endured well beyond the sentimentalism of a more liberal idealism of racial integration. Many decades after

King put Niebuhr to practice, the realities of racial injustice are still evident in America. Yet who can say that early in the 2000s there is not a vastly greater reach of justice in the land? Who even can deny that there has not been reconciliation, even the beginnings of a new interracial community in America?

King changed America a good century after Abraham Lincoln's liberating (and liberal) Emancipation Proclamation in 1863 failed to bring justice. Lincoln, Niebuhr, and King were among the occupants of the pulpit of America's civil religion. They, and hundreds of others of comparable if not equivalent importance, did not think as one. But they stood, as preachers of a kind, at the intersection of the nation's improbably high moral values and its impossibly common political hypocrisy. Lincoln, Niebuhr, and King, all three, and many others, sought justice; and all three understood that justice rolls down like waters and that the waters do necessary violence to the pastoral landscape.

Moral Man and Immoral Society makes a still vital contribution to the understanding of power and politics. The very thought is hard to take because it requires accepting the harsh realities that our ideals and values are not what we had hoped they would be. Love, such as it is, does not lead to justice. We cannot live together without a justice that includes all with whom we might join to form a communal society based on fairness that requires sacrifice. This is the problem Niebuhr addressed. Collective action toward justice is not a native-born gift. Human nature desires neither community nor justice. When we arrive collectively at any degree of justice, we arrive exhausted by the journey and bruised by the conflict.

Niebuhr's social ethic did not shrink from conflict, because he understood from the beginning of his career that perfectionism in ethics is a virtue of the individual, and even then it is seldom attained. Individuals who live by an ethic of love always come up against the limits of the selfishness within and without among others in the idealized community. In this world, love can never be perfect. It is human nature that creates the paradox. Beings of our species are not by nature opposed to others so much as they are excessively *for* themselves. This would be the problem to which Niebuhr would turn after *Moral Man and Immoral Society*.

4

sin,

self,

and

society

nature

and

destiny

of man

Niebuhr joined the faculty of the Union Theological Seminary under awkward circumstances. In 1928, the year he started, Union was easily the most prestigious graduate school of theology in the United States, perhaps in the world. Yet Niebuhr had had little advanced training. His only graduate degree was the one-year master's from Yale. He did not have the doctorate. His qualifications for a teaching post at a world-ranking institution were, at best, the national and international recognition of his public political and religious writings and the work in the Detroit years. He was not yet a scholar by any means. For this reason, in the first few years, he taught part-time and was paid off-budget, with the aid of an external patron, the writer and sponsor of left-liberal causes, Sherwood Eddy.[1] These no doubt were factors that persuaded the more accomplished scholars who would be his senior colleagues to accept the appointment, urged upon them by the school's new reform-minded president, Henry Sloane Coffin.

Niebuhr was, in effect, called to the teaching profession on the basis of a reputation rooted in his pastoral work—a perfectly legitimate basis for a position at Union, especially in the view of the school's new president, who meant to redirect Union toward training for ministry from an imbalance in favor of academic scholarship. Theological schools have traditionally employed pastors to teach students the practical arts of ministry, like preaching, missionary work, pastoral counseling. One well-known example, Harry Emerson Fosdick, the liberal pastor at nearby Riverside Church (and bête noire of American fundamentalists), was on the faculty during Niebuhr's time at Union. But it was then (as now) highly unusual at so highly ranked an institution as Union, with its close affiliation to Columbia University's world-renowned collegium of scholars, to call a man of so few academic qualifications for a position that so clearly entailed scholarship. Not only that, but Niebuhr's public record must have abraded the sensibilities of many on a faculty famous for its devotion to Social Gospel liberalism.

It did not take long for students and faculty to see what kind of a teacher and thinker Niebuhr was. In a short while, he had become one of the school's leading personages, and within two years he was unanimously appointed the Dodge Professor of Applied Christianity.[2] *Moral Man and Immoral Society* appeared in 1932, four years after the appointment. It certainly did not hurt his reputation in the Union community, but the sheer force of the man's mind and personal qualities had already won over any who may have doubted the merits of the appointment. On the other hand, it is not hard to imagine the reasons why a man of such determination and energy as Niebuhr's would have seized the opportunity of a prominent academic position that, as it turned out, could not possibly have been better suited to him.

Union at the time was the preeminent center for the scholarly study of theology and ethics in the United States and probably in the world. Then, too, Union and New York City together made a near perfect incubator for Niebuhr's thinking on religion and politics and an even better laboratory for their application and testing. Union's location in the Upper West Side next to Harlem, its proximity to the Council on Foreign Relations in Midtown, its institutional relations with the Jewish Theological Seminary and Columbia, the city's cultural and political ferment—all these factors made Union, especially in the 1930s, unique, as was the city itself. The great European centers were even more acutely embroiled in the economic and political catastrophes brought on by the Great War of 1914. New York, having been in the avant-garde of the Roaring Twenties, was now the epicenter of political and cultural adjustments to the end of that era.

One of Niebuhr's most astute historical insights was that Europe's nineteenth century collapsed in 1914, while America's held on until the crash of 1929. In the difference, America's attenuated isolation from the realities of the twentieth century lent it the time to both adjust to and dig in its heels against the reality of violence and uncertainty to come. This may be why when the worst of the long travail was over in 1945, Europe emerged the more realistic, while America lapsed into a schizophrenic delusion of grandeur frustrated by the hard realities of a changed world.[3]

Yet, returning to the 1930s, it would be easy to overlook the extent to which New York, as it had been for decades, was also America's gateway to Europe. Not only was Union Theological Seminary a leader in opening American doors to European theologians and religious leaders, but, as the crisis in Germany became more and more threatening to the safety of Jewish and Christian intellectuals, Union would be a haven for those fleeing Hitler.

Naturally, Niebuhr's German-American family history inclined him to serious political attention to the crisis, as it had prepared him for the scholarly study of the then-leading German-language theologians, principally the Swiss Emil Brunner and Karl Barth. He had met Brunner, who lectured at Union in the fall of 1928. Brunner would emerge late in the 1930s as a towering influence in modern theology. Two of Brunner's books—*Divine Imperative* (1932) and (especially) *Man in Revolt* (1937)—would be valued resources for Niebuhr's emerging position. Niebuhr met Barth only later.[4] It turned out that Niebuhr's study of the Swiss theologians led him to reconsider Pauline theology, which in turn opened up a fresh line of inquiry that led to his so-called orthodoxy.[5]

St. Paul himself, while a brilliant thinker able to reformulate the gospel narrative for the Hellenic world, was principally a pastor. He was the caretaker of the churches of the Christian Diaspora beyond its Jewish beginnings. Paul's writings were above all pastoral letters; and they were deeply personal. Before his conversion to Christianity, Paul had in fact been a persecutor of Christians. Afterward, as he preached the Gospel to the new, struggling churches, the evil he had perpetrated weighed constantly on him. In his Letter to the Romans (7:19), he wrote: "For the good that I would I do not: but the evil which I would not, that I do." Hence the paradox of sin against which Paul cautioned the earliest Christian believers by appeal to his own previous inability to control it in his own life. No other moral category is more central to Niebuhr's mature thinking, and preaching, than sin.

Whatever a skeptic might think of the idea of sin, and however many its meanings may be, it would be hard indeed to propose a notion more at odds with the liberal religion with which Niebuhr came to grips in the early years of his ministry. Sin, no doubt, had been a prominent reference point in his father's preaching, from which Niebuhr learned as a boy. By the 1920s, after some years of dealing with the social evils of industrial Detroit, his liberal faith in moral progress was all but gone. Still, the centrality of sin as an essential, if tragic, aspect of human nature would not surface until the 1930s in New York. Changes of mind of this magnitude are not matters of course. Whatever else it is, sin is about a deep resistance in the human condition to achieving the good the human spirit promises.

When an individual changes his thinking, and his moral attitude, the reasons for the change are never simple. For one, in the
1930s Niebuhr turned forty. He married in 1931, and within a few
years he and his wife, Ursula, welcomed their children, though
not without the grim experience of a miscarriage. In middle age,
Niebuhr began his fully adult life. Maturity and newfound intimacy have a way of deepening a man's understanding of life itself.

Then, too, the 1930s were a terrible shock to the American
soul. The economic collapse of 1929 and the wars looming in
Europe were sobering to all but the most naïve, able to shield
themselves from the realities of a radically altered world. The
United States in those years moved closer to the experience of the
wider world. Its Depression was global. Europe's Second World
War would again draw America in. Whatever innocence may
have lingered as nineteenth-century confidence in the free individual was crushed by the 1930s. The German-American Niebuhr's
family history and ethnic heritage predisposed him to think in
what today we call global terms. The crises of the 1930s focused
that disposition. Whatever the personal effects of marriage and
family life or of middle age, Niebuhr had long shown himself to
be able to focus his thinking in respect to (and for) the events in
the world about him. And as the 1930s wore on, from bad to
worse with only intermittent and slight improvement, his work
turned to the nuances of philosophical and human history and to
the question of human nature and its perversions.

Outside religious circles words like *sin* and *evil* are not
common. Inside, they are all too common, to the point of abuse.
Yet, as was his way, Niebuhr thought in and of the world as it is,

always with due regard for his own distinctive religious ideas. To any who have not tried to do this, it may sound like a relatively easy act of translation. But any who have recently attended religious services where homilies are offered will realize, if they are honest, that the act of translation is no mean trick, rarely well executed. And in no worldly culture, whatever its pretenses, is this trick harder to turn than in liberal ones in which progress toward a future good outcome is the definitive measure of worldly value. Even in the worst of times, the measure of the bad news is the promise of better times. Sin and evil are thus thorns in liberal flesh. Niebuhr was glad to poke away at the prevailing culture, but to do so he had to revise his thinking in ways that went well beyond borrowing from theological discourse in order to condemn secular evil.

All the more troubling is the fact that in America especially, sin suffers from its common association with sex—or, in that wonderful biblical word, fornication. Niebuhr took on sin, as such, but without covering its loins. Without lapsing into moralism on the subject, he realized that sex and sensuality were at the core of the Christian idea of sin. Sin, he thought, when not narrowly about sex, is about pride and selfishness:

> The climax of sexual union is also a climax of creativity and freedom. The element of sin in the experience is not due to the fact that sex is in any sense sinful as such. But once sin is presupposed, that is, once the original harmony of nature is disturbed by man's self-love, the instincts of sex are particularly effective tools for both the assertion of the self and flight from the self. This is what gives man's sex life the quality of uneasiness. It is both a vehicle of the primal sin of self-deification and the expression of an uneasy conscience, seeking to

escape from self by the deification of another. The deification of another is almost a literal description of many romantic sentiments in which attributes of perfection are assigned to the partner of love, beyond the capacities of any human being to bear, and therefore the cause of inevitable disillusionment.[6]

Niebuhr was thus quite clear that sin, though a term in the vocabulary of his religious background, was also a variant of what he considered the foremost moral problem of American political culture—pride and, one might say, self-glorification of the nation. Both aspects were, he came to argue, deeply embedded in ancient cultures of Europe and America. Sin by whatever name is as old as the Greeks, who, though hardly puritanical in the sense in which that term came to be used in the West, were just as concerned with the temptations of the bodily passions as were the divines of latter-day Calvinism and their heirs.

This confusion of sin with sex comes from an ancient and deeply ingrained idea that the human body is a vessel for the soul, from which comes the belief that sensual indulgence of the body harms the soul. This idea, while salient among certain puritanical religious traditions, is one that goes far back into ancient history, well before the Greeks, at least to the Mesopotamian myths of origin, including the expulsion of Adam and Eve from paradise for shamefully succumbing to their desire to know what only God knew. Eating the apple from the tree of knowledge is a metaphor for the ubiquity of overreaching intimacy.

In *Nature and Destiny of Man*, among other writings, Niebuhr explains that the association of sin with sensuality is also an explicit philosophical doctrine in the classical view of human nature of Aristotle, Plato, and the Stoics. Though they differed in important ways, these three were sources of the main traditions of Greek philosophy. They shared the general belief that mind and body were of different orders and that only the mind could be the source of human good. Though the belief can be worked in various ways, at the least it seems apparent that it had a powerful effect on the development of the religions of the modern West.

Puritanical thinking is present in all religions, as well as in quite a number of secular philosophies, but nowhere is it more pronounced than in the Abrahamic faiths—Christianity, Judaism, and Islam. At their extremes, elements of each denounce the pleasures of the body. Though some heretical branches of Islam are having a go for the top spot, Christianity retains the reputation for being the worst offender. Niebuhr came short of ranking the extremes but was clear on Christianity's collusion in a general cultural problem: "The compliance of conventional Christian morality with this essential identification of sin and sensuality has given modern critics of Christianity a partial justification for their belief that Christianity encourages prurience in its judgment of sexual problems and cruel self-righteousness on the part of the self-possessed and respectable members of the community toward those who have fallen into the obvious forms of sin."[7] Beyond the purely religious influences, there are many of the same effects in the secular side of its culture, which, as in Europe, derived as much from the Renaissance out of Greek and Judeo-Christian sources as from narrow puritanical Christianity.

If there is a masterwork among Niebuhr's many books, it would be *Nature and Destiny of Man*, which was the important achievement of his work in the 1930s. None other is quite so ambitious in its historical range; none so nuanced in its scholarship. The book is not perfect. Not everyone is persuaded by its claims. Some of its aspects (especially the unqualified use of the term *man*) will shock or puzzle readers in our day.

Still, no other book accounts more for why Niebuhr matters today. But the heart of the matter is not its exact political or social teachings (of which there are few) but its fresh exposition of what, in modern culture, is so little examined yet so apt to the political realities of our time, once again: sin. As he lived through, and thought about, the disastrous events of the twentieth century, sin and evil assumed an ever more acute salience in the history before him—a salience that merited the scholarly seriousness he devoted to the subject in the 1930s.

To read the writings of Reinhold Niebuhr over the ten or so years after his appointment to the Dodge professorship is to be astonished at the learning. He was not, and never claimed to be, a pure scholar of theological history (as were Brunner and Barth). Nor was he a social historian of American theology and religion (as was his brother Richard at Yale). Reinhold's scholarship even when applied to the history of Christian social ethics as in *Interpretation of Christian Ethics* was unswervingly directed to social and political ethics, not to theology.[8] His examples—social as well as theological—were always drawn from fine points of biblical and historical sources. If pure scholars quibble with his representations of the facts of theological history (and many have), the overriding quality of Niebuhr's writings in the 1930s is the range and depth of his knowledge of the long history of Greek philosophy, early and medieval Christianity, and modern social, religious, and political thought. Niebuhr's mastery of so many subjects, if at times imperfect, was acutely impressive given that his life as a scholar of these subjects had begun so few years before.[9]

As in the Detroit years, Niebuhr kept up his political work and his itinerant preaching, to which he added numerous and regular open houses for students at Union and a new teaching program on topics for which he had had scant preparation, while taking on the added responsibility for scholarship and learning he had forgone in the Detroit years. As before, much of the scholarship was pursued according to his long-held habit of staying up late to write and read. Summer holidays in the Berkshires served as an annual work retreat (though not without still numerous social and political engagements).[10]

Niebuhr's *Nature and Destiny of Man*, the first volume of which appeared in 1941, was the fresh full fruit of these continuing and added labors. The occasion for writing the book was his 1939 series of Gifford lectures on natural theology in Scotland—possibly the most distinguished lectureship in the world and certainly the most important on religious topics since their inception in 1888. William James's *Varieties of Religious Experience* was a Gifford lecture (in 1900–1902), as was Alfred North

Whitehead's *Process and Reality* (in 1927–28). Other lecturers have been Josiah Royce, Albert Schweitzer, Karl Barth, Paul Tillich, Mary Douglas, and Noam Chomsky. For Niebuhr to have been selected for these (usually) yearlong lectures just more than a decade after he had begun his career at Union is still another indication of how quickly his scholarly reputation was established and how influential his thinking had become.

While the Gifford lectures were originally meant to deal with natural theology, many of the lecturers were neither theologians nor thinkers particularly committed to naturalism of any kind. Still, a hint of Niebuhr's seriousness of purpose is that he chose a topic, the nature and destiny of man, that demanded a probative knowledge of human nature and naturalism, subjects he had not previously explored in any great detail.

Moral Man had been unique for its political and social theories that grew out of Niebuhr's disenchantment with liberal religion in America. It was directed at the crisis in the West prompted by the Great War and the economic collapse of 1929. *Nature and Destiny of Man* was written later in the same crisis, but the 1939 lectures were cast against the ever more severe realities of a second war in Europe and the shredding of liberal politics before the onslaught of fascisms. In fact, by the end of the fall term's lectures in 1939, his family had already returned home as Niebuhr finished his Gifford lectures—the noise of war literally ringing in his ears.[11]

Nature and Destiny of Man was shaped by two quite different historical sources. One, from centuries of human thought, was the question posed by the Gifford lectures themselves. What is human nature and what might be the place of religion in it? The other, from the moment then at hand in 1939, after a quarter-century of war and economic crisis, with fascism pressing toward the certainty of another global war was: What is the fate of man? *Nature and Destiny of Man* was as much rooted in ancient wisdom as it was informed by the moral and political urgency of the times. Still, there is a jarring quality to the book itself, not least of which is its attention to sin.

The deep coupling of sin with sex in the nether parts of Western culture has done a good bit of damage—of which the trivialization of sin is the most grave. Sin is a serious matter and a powerful drive that can disrupt all aspects of human behavior. Sex can be sin, thus, not by the deed but by, in St. Paul's phrase, its effect on the "inward man"—an effect so potent as to render human intelligence feeble before it. Concupiscence, not coitus, is at the heart of the problem. Strong bodily desires are natural. Without them animal life would wither. Sin thus has to do with the part of human nature that transcends elemental animal passions.

Whatever may be unique and special about humankind, human beings begin and end as nature's beings. They are born animals. Like all other animals, they die. When they do, what remains are nature's leavings. From dust to dust! In the modern West, the problem is that almost no one stops to think about the deeper facts of life and death. Men and women, having been taught from the cradle not to play with themselves, generally live as if they did not have bodies that must obey the rules of nature. It may well be, and almost surely is, that sex, like violence, is a natural impulse necessary to the survival of animals in more ways than the obvious one. Neutered dogs will hump each other. What are they thinking when they sniff those dead balls? On these subjects, if on any, they are not thinking as humans think.

Human thinking, as it has come to be understood, begins in self-consciousness. The ability to form objects in the mind seems to be lacking in preverbal infants, who are at best able to experience feelings prompted by vague presences that in time are understood to be a source of their pleasures. An infant may enjoy the sensual pleasure of human touch, but only when she comes to use language does she think, and then very slowly.

Language allows even the toddler to manipulate his world, such as it may be. He wants to move about in it, to pursue its pleasures. His most subtle movement is that of pointing his body, even his fingers, toward someone or something. In his indexing of objects and beings he is developing the capacity to be someone. Pointing is language, however crude. When the child crawls with determination toward some object he is, if not thinking as such, at least semiconscious of his desires. Thus begins self-consciousness—the early experiments when objects are prelude to the self as object unto itself.

Jacques Lacan, the famous French psychoanalyst, may be right that the crucial moment for the infant is the mirror stage, when she looks at herself in some reflecting surface there to see a creature so much more whole and real than any living self can be.[12] And even if Lacan is wrong (or not completely right), who has not had the experience of disappointing herself—disappointing, often deeply, her sense of who she thinks she is in respect to what, truth be told, she fails to do? Our actual selves, as we live them, are always less than we suppose they ought to be. This is the most fundamental natural fact of human being. The question is how to manage the shortcoming. This is where, according to Niebuhr, sin comes in. Sin is much more about a cavernous spiritual disappointment and how it is dealt with than about the frailties of the body.

Still, we must wonder: What is meant by human nature? How do human beings in their particularities come to terms with their nature? A nature arises among self-conscious beings when they (which is to say, we) engage in the practice of inventing or discovering the categories by which members come to share a common, perhaps even universal, understanding of their relations with all others of the category. It is natural for those party to such a species to locate themselves in relation to some meaningful others. When human societies trace their origins back to a legendary being or primordial state of their nature—Adam, Gilgamesh, Romulus, Wakan Tanka, George Washington, Olodumare, Man in the Original Position, Ronald Reagan, Sponge Bob, others—they are claiming for themselves a right to belong to a nature endowed by and for them.

There are those who would call the attempt to understand human nature a search for meaning. But this sharpens the point a bit too finely. Meaning, when found, is found half-wittingly and never in and of itself. Plus which it is always found *with* others, notwithstanding their inconsideration of us and we of them. Humans are capable of thinking, but most of them are not very thoughtful. Their native incompetence at considering the feelings of others is somehow part and parcel of their thoughtlessness. And never are they more thoughtless than when they so brusquely say and do things that pull us into the realization that we do as they do.

The very idea that our gift of self-consciousness is meant for use in considering the consciousness of others may seem preposterous at any given moment. But in time, it is hard to get around—if only because it is in our nature, somehow, to have a nature of which we are conscious, which consciousness we resist. We are, thereby, creatures free to be unique among all other beings, but bound in practice to be anything but. Even in the secular consciousness, the Protestant paradox confounds. One of the reasons we don't get the sex we desire as often as we would like, or with whom we would like, is that we may well have a record of being unable to consider others for what they want from us. More often than not we fail to touch the other in ways that let her know that we care who she is and what she needs. Sex is but one of life's playing fields in which we touch, or fail to touch, the others we need and want.

Sin is about self; but there can be no self outside a species. Selves are members of a category, and when it comes to being human the most urgent category, thought Niebuhr, is community:

> Community is an individual as well as social necessity; for the individual can realize himself only in intimate and organic relation with his fellowmen. Love is therefore the primary law of his nature; and brotherhood the fundamental requirement of his social existence.[13]

Selves understand who they are only when they understand *what* they are. This is not easy, because such an understanding is almost impossible to come by. This is not because we are too stupid to get it; or because it is too far beyond human knowledge (though well it may be). It is because we have our nature as individuals less by knowing than by experiencing being with others—the very others our thoughtlessness keeps us from.

Like most deep things, human nature, being the consideration of what is common to the species, is in practice many things at once. Naturally occurring human beings are no one thing all at once. We are clearly animals. We need everything our dogs need, though our dogs are more gifted at getting what they need without a lot of talk. Yet even when we talk ourselves into getting what we need, we seldom are completely satisfied. The new dress wrinkles. The new car dents. The sex does not meet the fantasy. The cot in the shelter is next to a loud drunk. When and if wisdom dawns, we learn that what we needed was in fact what we wanted—not at all the same thing.

It is human nature that there will always be something out there beyond the acquisition of needs or the satiation of the desires that leaves us unsettled. Again, Niebuhr: "The essential homelessness of the human spirit is the ground of all religion; for the self which stands outside itself and the world cannot find the meaning of life in itself or the world."[14] If we cannot find the meaning we desire within, in the inward man, then we can only look for it beyond the immediately available. We seek a home with others. We are homeless by nature—a fact of human existence that requires us always to look beyond. In the looking we encounter impulses laden with temptations to settle for less—for anything near about that we can grasp and manage. The beyond we seek cannot be grasped by the neck. Life thus is disappointing because to be human is to desire what is out of reach. For thinking creatures with creative spirits this is a hard reality to stomach. We try all too logically to get around it.

But death gets in the way. We know we will die. A few die well. Most die hard because they live in a culture that encourages them not to come face to face with the fact of life's limits. Dying well can be about religion, but not necessarily; some of little or no faith die well. Either way, the moment of our death is something that must be dealt with. But dealing with death involves a consideration that, on the face of it, contradicts everything we trust in this life. We who experience ourselves so vividly, for better or worse, will one day disappear into if not a nothingness, at least an unknowable whatever. The prospect is hard, if not impossible, to think.

Human beings think. Thinking begins with self-consciousness. So humans think first about themselves. Thus since all of us experience our births (even in the dim confusion of our preverbal state), our actual births are not in the moment of being snatched from a womb. Each of us is born as a self when she becomes aware that she has a self—that is, a quality of being distinct from the welter of dark and light, silence and noise about her. Descartes was right at least on this. The original clear and distinct idea was that in thinking we are something.

Sin is about self, but self is about consciousness, thus thought; and thought is what allows us to think about our end.[15] Sin thus is a species problem—the problem, as Niebuhr put it, of being more than our nature because we can think ourselves; and, at the same time, being limited by the reality that we will die. Dogs are what dogs are. Man, among the animals, is a neither/nor creature. Dogs do not sin; men do. Niebuhr put this as well as anyone since Søren Kierkegaard:

> Man, being both free and bound, both limited and limitless, is anxious. Anxiety is the inevitable concomitant of the paradox of freedom and finiteness in which man is involved. Anxiety is the internal precondition of sin. It is the inevitable spiritual state of man, standing in the paradoxical situation of freedom and finiteness.[16]

We are who we are because of *what* we are—chiefly, creatures who will die and who know it.

How we live is determined to a stout degree by how we come to terms with this dilemma. But one never comes to terms with life and death as a solitary self. We must deal with the others about us if we are to remain human. We would like others to be better than they are—more considerate of us; but whatever they are, we must take them on their own terms. There, precisely, is the riddle of human being. We are individual selves, yet we depend on others who are not by nature well disposed toward us, at least not uniformly or consistently so. No matter which way you slice it, the irony is that individual humans are not particularly well suited for the life with one another on which they depend.

We require the presence of others because, as William James was among the first in modern times to say, we have selves only to the degree that others recognize us.[17] This may lead, James said, to our having many selves—that is, many *social* selves by which we adjust ourselves to the several others with whom we must contend whether near at hand or in passing. Yet the problem of social inconsideration enters still again.

What is in it for others to recognize (much less consider) us? If they and we do not, then we as individuals and the community as a whole will not survive. Often they do it only because they, on their side, accept the responsibility of recognizing others as an assurance that there will be ones who recognize them. What goes around comes around when it comes to social recognitions and the necessary company of others. Even monks sworn to lives of solitude and silence recognize the brother who farts during compline.

We might say that society is the most unlikely of human conventions while also being the most urgently necessary. The nature of human being is that collective life is built up in spite of our unique capacity for selfishness. Whether or not this means we can say that societies by *their* natures are selfish is a tough question. But if Niebuhr is right on this score, then he is also right to add: "A distinction between group pride and the egotism of individuals is necessary, furthermore, because the pretensions and claims of a collective or social self exceed those of the individual ego. The group is more arrogant, hypocritical, self-centered in the pursuit of its ends than the individual. An inevitable moral tension between individual and group morality is therefore created."[18] As was already evident in *Moral Man and Immoral Society*, Niebuhr understood very well that there is an important moral difference between individuals and societies. Whatever the semantic slippage involved in "group egotism," we know for a fact that, if what you are looking for is love, you are more likely to get it from an individual than a society. Societies, by contrast, have a hard enough time doing anything decent without pressure of some kind. The best societies can do is occasionally, and not always happily, spread a little justice around—and this usually, as Niebuhr says, only when they are coerced.

Sin is about self; self is about life with others; sin, thereby, is a social thing; and social things are at least as self-involved as are individuals. Therefore, far from being about sex, sin is about self; and because selves are about social needs and necessities, there is nowhere one can go where there is no sin.[19] Why and how this may be so remains to be seen.

If Niebuhr matters to times other than his own because of his theory of sin and human nature, then for him sin's necessary relation to human nature determines our fate. Fate, like sin, may seem an idea from another time. But the reality is that beginning with the experiences Niebuhr himself lived through and dealt with in the middle decades of the twentieth century, the world as he knew it, like the one we now must understand, seems so clearly to be *fated*—to be, that is, pushed and pulled by forces more powerful than the best human intentions.

The better part of a century after Niebuhr began his ministry in Detroit in 1915, the high hopes of European moderns have been dashed. He lived and thought during the most terrible of times for modern sensibilities. Still, since Niebuhr's day, progress has been made, miraculous progress, in science, medicine, engineering, and technology. Just the same, in the twenty-first century being human is not the robust prospect that, a century before, it was thought to be; nor even what, after the wars and economic failures had lifted in the 1950s, people thought it would again become.

Nature and Destiny of Man is Niebuhr's statement of the deeper reasons behind the frustrations of our destiny by the uncertainties of our nature. The lessons of this book are, however, difficult to take in. For one, Niebuhr, the evangelical preacher, insists that we humans are not, and cannot be, as supreme as we believe ourselves to be. Yet as theological as this insistence might be—beginning, of course, with the commandment not to worship other gods before Yahweh—the theological principle is also remarkably good sociology.

To be certain, neither sociology nor any other of the social sciences has taken the point Niebuhr makes. This is because sociologies of all kinds are so deeply embedded in the false faith and futile fate of modernity's belief in reason, "man," and progress. Another reason why there were once, and still are, Atheists for Niebuhr is that his religious views, though firm, even harsh, were offered with such a clear and balanced grasp of the nature of secular modernity. So much of what passes today as evangelical religion in America is openly, even aggressively, hostile to what some evangelicals call secular humanity. Niebuhr's view on the subject is that pagan and secular traditions are part of human history, especially in the West, and that the fate of modern man cannot be understood apart from that history. At the same time, a particularly powerful aspect of his religious views is that the Beyond inspired by, but limiting of, human freedom, while to him a religious factor, is also part of deep structural grammar that articulates mankind's historical fate.

Niebuhr was not a historian in the technical sense. But he was unfailingly historical. He did not deal in the ferreting out of the empirical facts of the human condition. But he was soberly factual in the sense of always examining his ethical and religious ideas against the evidence of history. He did not, however, take history on its own terms. Niebuhr's interpretative scheme was systematic and well enough grounded. His method was based on his own fair but ironic assessment of the prior sources, religious and secular, as they viewed their histories, *and* on his independent inspection of the events of his time.[20] At the same time, Niebuhr's thinking was historical in a way that allowed him to draw judgments from the past that illuminated the present with a sense of human destiny—from which those coming after him could draw their own conclusions as to the (never linear) trajectory of mankind's fate. This is the way destinies work in history—one time leads to another, awkwardly.

In a nutshell, Niebuhr's method was, as many have noted, dialectical without being Hegelian. G. W. F. Hegel (1770–1831), the great German philosopher, famously proposed that history moves by the opposing actions of thesis and antithesis resolving in a new synthesis, from which the dialectic of contradictions begins anew. Niebuhr's view was that history never resolves history's contradictions, because man's nature is both free and bound—making the human individual able to see, often to fashion new social and technical stages, but also *unable* to see beyond to her historically real failures. In some ways the willingness to think of the human as both creative and arrogant—as free to make prog-ress and stupid as to the limits of progress—is a method that modernity resists, yet one that moderns and postmoderns could use, if only they would.

In practice, Niebuhr's method, while religiously based, is broadly applicable. We have already seen an instance of it in the way Niebuhr defined man in the first place—as a figure in modern history shaped dialectically by the classical, Christian, and modern theories of man. Two of the three are predomi-nantly, but not wholly, pagan and secular. But Niebuhr did not do as latter-day evangelicals would. He did not set the Christian view over against the other two. Christian thinking is as suscep-tible to corruption as any other—in particular by slipping, on the one side, into an ahistorical orthodoxy in which man is in effect nothing before God and, on the other, into a prideful historicism in which God is a figment of man's liberal fantasy that history is progress.[21] Thus, for one example, Marxism is put forth as the equivalent of liberalism, including Christian liber-alism, in that both believe, by different means, that history can and will turn out for the good.

Virtually everything Niebuhr taught and wrote after 1932 led to *Nature and Destiny of Man*, the book that justifies the notion that he was neo-orthodox. Yet there is an important difference between orthodoxy as such and Niebuhr's new formulation of biblical and evangelical principles. That difference is nowhere more apparent than in the way he thought through his criticism of liberalisms in terms ever more harsh than those he used against orthodoxies. This was another expression of the workings of his version of the Protestant principle. Niebuhr was a neither/nor thinker who refused to settle on any final solution that failed to acknowledge the determined fate of man—that he will die and he knows it but cannot face it. Liberals believe too naïvely in the boundless evolution of human progress, which to his tastes was ahistorical.

Niebuhr's method suffered its faults, to be sure. In particular, he sometimes defines the opposing instances a bit too strongly— as if classical, modern, and biblical were pure types. Yet on balance, in the analysis of particular issues and concepts the subtlety emerges—and especially so when he attends to the historical record.

Nothing in the years Niebuhr prepared himself for *Nature and Destiny* better illustrates the merits of his method than the crisis of 1929. With the Depression, capitalism's chickens came home to roost: "The social mechanisms of a commercial civilization, in short, veil the brutal realities of social life and obscure the factors of egoistic and imperial impulse which determine it to a large degree."[22] Niebuhr's idea that the innocent nineteenth century first cracked in 1914 in Europe, then came to its final collapse in 1929 could have occurred only to a mind trained on history. Depression, however devastatingly widespread its effects, was not an event among others. It was a symptom of a larger crisis, one that would not be resolved by a restoration of the global economy. All structural crises are historical. They thus reveal themselves in different periods according to differing rules of historical formation. Yet in the work of the 1930s, Niebuhr came also to the realization that the crisis of his time was an aspect of human destiny—not a predetermined inevitably but an outcome with real and specific historical qualities that, once unveiled, can be understood as a fate occasioned by human pride and selfishness.

To think of man's historical destiny as Niebuhr thought of it, it is necessary to return to Augustine of Hippo (354–430 C.E.), the brilliant bishop of North Africa who influenced Niebuhr's thinking in the years after *Reflections on the End of an Era* in 1934.

Augustine provided Niebuhr a constructive way around his frustrations with liberalism and disappointments with Marxism. Beyond Niebuhr's primary reliance on the Christian Scripture (a reliance facilitated by what seems to have been a near photographic memory of its key passages), Augustine helped Niebuhr solidify his mature theories of the nature and destiny of man.

Historically, Augustine was the cultural vault that kept Pauline thought safe during the millennium-plus of Catholic Christendom—if not from Constantine's division of the Empire in 324, at least from the sack of Rome in 410 to Luther's *Ninety-five Theses* on October 31, 1517.[23] It was the Catholic legitimacy of Augustine that vouchsafed Paul's psychology of the inward man to Martin Luther in the sixteenth century and to the other Reformers who defied ecclesiastical authority in favor of the believer's personal faith. Yet as the history of religious wars in the long sixteenth century and in the modern era as a whole have shown, the contributions of Paul through Augustine to the Reformation were more than a psychology of modern individualism. A leading interpreter of Augustine, Charles Norris Cochrane (who influenced Niebuhr's view of Augustine), said, remarkably: "The discovery of personality was, at the same time, the discovery of history."[24] Disconcerting though it may be, this simple formula is loaded with implications.

If one posits, as did Paul, an authoritative but limited inward man, then, as in Augustine, the self or personality is of necessity a trinity of movements—memory, understanding, and will:

> So when one talks about these three things in a person, disposition, learning, practice, one judges the first according to what he can do with his *memory*, his *understanding*, and his *will*; one estimates the second according to what he actually has in his memory and understanding, and where he has got to with his will to study; the third however is to be found in the use the will now makes of what the memory and understanding hold, whether it refers them to something else or whether it takes delight in them as ends in themselves. . . . *These three then, memory, understanding, and will, are not three lives but one life, nor three minds but one mind.*[25]

Augustine's commingling of memory, understanding, and will in one mind and one self is a sharp break with the Greek (particularly Platonic) theory of mind-body dualism in which the particular mind was an instance of an eternal form (hence the moral corruptions of the body).[26] In today's terms the Platonic ethic leads to a virtue ethic in which the individual is good to the extent that her character approximates the eternal good, hence the Catholic idea that the Christian is meant to emulate Christ, against whom the Church judges the state of his soul, which is saved only by grace dispensed by the priestly class.

Once Augustine made the move to insert *will* into the mix between *understanding* and *memory*, the effect was to reformulate the self or mind in the image of the divine Trinity—ultimately a very Protestant notion in that the Christ is not the eternal form of the Good but the historical actor (a messiah, as Paul put it) who introjects God's will into human history so that man can understand himself only through memory. Memory thus is the unfathomable well of all that passes through experience. Memory, when active, is an understanding not just of events but of *human* events—both the creative and failed activities of the will. The historical self thereby transcends what it remembers by understanding more than it can know. Thus from the point of view of religious history, the Protestant Communion is a memorial service (in contrast to the Roman Eucharist, which is meant to be an incarnation of the divine body and blood in the present). Hence Cochrane's insight into Augustine's salvaging of what St. Paul called the inward man from its Platonic strains by asserting as the biblical truth the deep psychology of human history. For Paul the inward man was the corollary of his famous confessional statement of man's inability to resist sin: "For the good that I would I do not: but the evil which I would not, that I do. Now if I do that I would not, it is no more I that do it, but sin that dwelleth in me" (Romans 7:19–20).[27] Here the classical idea of the inward man becomes an astonishingly modern self-psychology.

If history is to be more real than a grand narrative and more concrete than an abstract working out of a natural or supernatural plan, then history must be the sphere of human willing, but a willing always in debt to memory, always inclined toward understanding—always thus a collective sphere of self-reflection.

History, like personality, is thus imperfect, as likely to fail as not. History, like the human soul, is marked by sin, an abiding uncertainty that presents itself as an impulse to do and to be more than man can do or be.

But how did this line of thinking open up over so long a historical journey? What specifically were the historical markers that led Paul, himself Platonic to a degree, to pursue an implicit theory of history—a theory that would be picked up four centuries later by Augustine to invent a presciently modern idea of the historical self, to be picked up in turn another four centuries later by Niebuhr? The long story turns on Augustine, without whom it might have been lost.

In the popular imagination Augustine's *Confessions* (397–98 C.E.) may be the best known text. For philosophers *On the Trinity* (400–416) is the most important treatise on the psychology of mind since the Greeks and probably the single most important classical work on the psychology of the self. Still, in the realm of historical and theological analysis, Augustine's greatest work is *The City of God* (413–26)—a mammoth book of subtle philosophical reflection and delicate sociological judgment on the end of the world into which he had been born.

Rome, from its earliest, if legendary, beginnings in 753 B.C.E., grew to become one of the major global powers of its day—of any day, for that matter. First as the Republic, which collapsed upon the assassination of Julius Caesar in 44 B.C.E., then as the Empire established by Augustus in 28 B.C.E., Rome came to dominate its world. Under Trajan (r. 98–117 C.E.), Rome ruled some six million square kilometers. In the ancient world only the Persian Empire under Darius and Xerxes (550–330 B.C.E.) and the Han Dynasties (206 B.C.E.–220 C.E.) were greater in size. Alexander's Macedonian Empire (356–323 B.C.E.) lasted but a generation, the Persians but two centuries, the Hans four. Rome was an imperial force for roughly a millennium—thence: Rome, the Eternal City.

Augustine lived in the aftershock of Rome's long decline, dramatized by Alaric's sack of Rome in 410 C.E.. But the agony of it all continued for years after that. The vastness of Rome's reach and the durability of its power dwarf the roughly half-millennium of the modern West from Europe's first colonizing ventures around 1500 C.E. down to our time, more or less. Still, the relatively sudden depletion of Rome's power makes the modern world's 9/11 seem a trifle. When Rome fell, few doubted that it was over. Endings of these kinds, whatever their moment of irruption, can usually be anticipated only in hindsight, seldom at the time of their occurrence.

What did Augustine take from the late history of a declining Empire that could have been of such importance to Niebuhr in the years he called the end of an era? In an offhand remark during a lecture in 1960 Niebuhr proposed that Augustine's creativity was greatly enhanced by, perhaps even indebted to, the devastating collapse of the world about him.[28] The falling away of taken-for-granted cultures and structures like those of Eternal Rome can have the effect of challenging seemingly immutable values. What may have been true of Augustine applies just as well to Niebuhr. Self-aggrandizing civilizations and cultures are sooner or later contradicted by their own histories.

This, precisely, is what Niebuhr took from Augustine—a theory of civilizations that so surpasses the inevitability of human history as to render even the grandest of its achievements brittle from the start. Such a theory is *not*, however, a cyclical theory of history that, with daring ignorance of the irregularities of social structures, insists that all empires, states, and civilizations rise and fall according to historical necessity. The appeal of historical theories of the cyclical kind is that they *seem* to hold up to the evidence—of which the decline and fall of the Roman Empire is the preeminent subject of fascination. It is true, of course, that the Persians, the Hans, the Romans, the Iberians, the British, and all the others enjoyed clear and traceable trajectories to their global powers; true also that, whether short or long, their declines can be marked. But the markings along a purported line of progressive rise spilling over into a sickening fall are always an after-the-fact historical narrative—true only if pushed too far by such suprahistorical abstractions as a natural law of economic and social fluctuations or any one of the pure cyclical ideologies of social change.

What Niebuhr took from Augustine above all others is that history is subject to muses beyond its internal dynamics. What makes for history, both believed, is not of this world. Clearly, both drew this conclusion from their Christian values and biblical ideas. Just as clearly, this fact alone may preclude a fair hearing among nonbelievers. Yet before dismissing them, one might approach the question of history from another angle—the one both Augustine and Niebuhr took from their religion.

Hayden White, the theorist of history (and not a theologian of any kind), has distinguished five "levels" of thinking in the writing of history: *chronicle* (description of the series of events), *story* (the narrative elements found in the events), *plot* (how the historian retells the story), *argument* (the historian's interpretation of the meaning of the emplotted stories), and *ideology* (the ideological elements at work in the historical work).[29] If one were to take the fifth, ideology, in a relatively neutral sense to mean the precise ways the interests of the historian influence the argument, storytelling, even reading of the chronicle, then it is not hard to see that histories partake of the events of which they write. Hence the failure of cyclical and other abstract theories of history is that they stipulate a structure to history that cannot be described by the facts of history. All overgeneralized implicit or explicit theories of the way history works suffer this defect. None more so than the modern liberal theories of history that stipulate modernity itself as the progressive outcome of all that came before and thus as the destiny of the human race. Abraham Lincoln's 1862 pronouncement of the American Union as the last best hope on earth was good politics, fine rhetoric, necessary unto the times, but also a classically modernist theory of history. The present is prelude to the future. This, of course, was not on Augustine's mind in the 420s, but it suited Niebuhr's historical and ethical sensibilities late in the 1930s.

Augustine's *City of God* is a book like few others. It is at once: a commentary on the decline of Rome (hence, a social historical note, if not a full-blown sociology of civilizations), a summary of the deep structural pasts of Greco-Roman philosophy and culture, a comparative exposition of Judeo-Christian teachings, a theory of history as such, and a book that demands of its readers an ability to range across centuries and fields of learning few then or now possess. The full title of the book, *On the City of God Against the Pagans*, reveals that it is also a polemic attacking the reigning culture of Augustine's day much as Niebuhr did in his.

The Latin *civis* translates as *city*, to be sure, but its meaning invites the idea of *civilization* or, in effect, *empire*. Rome was the Eternal City because it was, both in Roman times and under the Holy Roman Empire after Charles the Great in 800 C.E., the visible center of a global construct. Thus Augustine's *City of God* meant, by the juxtaposition to the City of Man (the City of Pagans), to expose the decrepitude of all empires. Just as much, it was far more than a straightforward attack on the profanations of the powers of this world. Augustine begins:

> I have taken upon myself the task of defending the glorious City of God against those who prefer their own gods to the Founder of that City. . . . Therefore I cannot refrain from speaking of the city of this world, a city which aims at dominion, which holds nations in enslavement, but is itself dominated by that very lust of domination.[30]

At first impression, if it is possible to take an impression from roughly 500,000 words, the book seems to offer a defense of Christianity against paganism. It does, but not as one might suppose. Nor is *City of God* an early entry in the decline–and-fall-of-Rome genre. What makes this book a serious theory of history that merits attention in and beyond Christian traditions is its violation of expectations. While believers would likely be offended by the idea, the argument level of Augustine's history of Rome offers a thoroughly viable exposition of the inherent corruption of all empires:

> Is it reasonable, is it sensible, to boast of the extent and grandeur of empire, when you cannot show that men lived in happiness, as they passed their lives amid the horrors of war, among the shedding of men's blood—whether the blood of enemies or fellow citizens—under that shadow of fear and amid the terror of ruthless ambition? The only joy to be attained had the fragile brilliance of glass, a joy outweighed by the fear that it may be shattered in a moment.[31]

Could Romans in 410 C.E. have experienced the sack of Rome as moderns experienced the fall of the twin towers on the morning of September 11, 2001? When social forms considered eternal or inherently good and true snap—or as was the case both in 410 and 2001, appear to be snapping—the shattering has a televisual effect. The image gets inside the brain in ways that pass all understanding.

Augustine's theory of history was that all kingdoms of this world are fragile. Not in and of itself a startling observation, unless it is combined (as it was) with a theory of political power as domination:

> Remove justice, and what are kingdoms but gangs of criminals on a large scale? What are criminal gangs but petty kingdoms? A gang is a group of men under the command of a leader, bound by a compact of associates, in which the plunder is divided according to an agreed convention. . . . If this villainy wins so many recruits from the ranks of the demoralized that it acquires territory, establishes a base, captures cities and subdues peoples, it then openly arrogates to itself the title of kingdom, which is conferred on it in the eyes of the world, not by the renouncing of aggression but by the attainment of

impunity. . . . For it was a witty and truthful rejoinder which was given by a captured pirate to Alexander the Great. The king asked the fellow, "What is your idea, in infesting the sea?" And the pirate answered, with uninhibited insolence, "The same as yours, in infesting the earth! But because I do it with a tiny craft, I'm called a pirate; because you have a mighty navy, you're called an emperor."[32]

Augustine's theory of history is, among other things, a theory of imperial power and corruption. Enter Niebuhr.

There few books I know that compare as favorably to *City of God* as Niebuhr's *Nature and Destiny of Man*. Books like these are important because they were so quick to a historical moment that they reset the calculus of what man's human destiny might be. If, in Augustine's case, all political authority is imperial domination, then not only must the values of the reigning civilizations be questioned, but so too must be the nature of man as such. It is one thing to come at the theme, as Augustine obviously does, from the point of view of the City of God, but something even more to pursue it in terms that, beyond the author's disposition, are so apt to a general understanding of the issues at hand.

Niebuhr's *Nature and Destiny of Man*, great though it may have been, differs, however, from Augustine's *City of God* in two ways. As a writer, Augustine was a poet. Niebuhr was simply eloquent. Also, the magnitude of the historical crisis Augustine applied himself to was, at the time of his writing and since, considered paradigmatic; while Niebuhr's crisis of industrial capitalism is not, even now, decades later, recognized for what it may well have been.

Before coming to the question of whether the crisis of the modern era *should* be thought of as comparable to the collapse of classical civilization, a comparison of *Nature and Destiny of Man* and *City of God* unmistakably suggests the extent to which Niebuhr used not only Augustine's ideas but even his plot plan (as Hayden White would put it). Niebuhr's motif may have been less overtly historical and keyed on a somewhat different line of argument, but the comparison holds. As Charles Norris Cochrane concludes, Augustine's theory of history is a "history of prophecy; i.e., its true significance lies not in the past, nor in the present, but in the future, the life of 'the world to come.'" More pungently Cochrane also says of the implications of Augustine's idea of human history:

> Properly understood, history is the record of a struggle, not for the realization of material or ideal values but for the materialization, embodiment, the registration in consciousness of real values, the values of truth, beauty, and goodness which are thus so to speak thrust upon it as the very condition of its life and being. In these terms and in these terms alone can the secular effort of the human spirit be explained and justified, for only thus does it become intelligible.[33]

It is relatively easy to see just how important Cochrane was as a guide to Niebuhr's appreciation of Augustine and, in turn, why Augustine's writing (remembering also the importance the theory of the self and history in *On the Trinity*) was so profoundly important to Niebuhr's thinking.

What, then, was Niebuhr's conclusion about the destiny of man? The answer is hinted at in *Moral Man*, Niebuhr's first book of

Christian realism, and developed in his critique of modern economic culture in *Reflections on the End of an Era.*

Nature and Destiny of Man could then also be said to be the completion of a cycle of writings—a text that would provide the philosophical underpinnings of what would become Niebuhr's settled position on the modern era. If this, then one is bound to admit to another of the ways Niebuhr's work, while brilliantly apt to the current situation (which I take to be an extension of his), fell short of Augustine's *City of God.* It took Niebuhr three books to approach what Augustine achieved in one—a theory of political realism, a diagnosis of the historical crisis of the day, and a systematic theory of history and human nature. At the same time it might be said that what Niebuhr achieved in just more than a decade (1932–41) took Augustine a good fifteen years (413–27). Still, Niebuhr's greatest work falls short of Augustine's to the degree to which the fall of Rome was more salient an event early in the fifth century than the slippage and dislocations of the modern era were in the mid-twentieth.

Niebuhr's introduction to the second book of *Nature and Destiny* is, in its way, more troubling to those with distaste for the parochial:

Historical religions are . . . by their very nature prophetic-Messianic. They look forward at first to a point in history and finally towards an *eschaton* (end) which is also the end of history, where the full meaning of life and history will be disclosed. . . . The basic distinction between historical and non-historical religions *and cultures* may thus be succinctly defined as the difference between those which expect and those who did not expect a Christ. . . . A Christ is expected wherever history is thought of as a realm of fragmentary revelations of a purpose and power transcending history, point to a fuller disclosure of that purpose and power.[34]

Strictly speaking, from the Greek, a *Christos* is an "anointed one" or, simply, a messiah—one who comes into history to account for what history cannot reveal to itself. The arrogance of Christian doctrine is its claim that its messianic figure was *the* Christ. All historical religions and cultures that refrain from thinking of history as self-fulfilling and self-explaining expect a Christ—at least in theoretical principle. This surely includes the Abrahamic religions of the West and many cultures of the ancient world—notably the Persian, Babylonian, and Egyptian. That the ideal of a "messiah" has been appropriated by one uniquely Western religion, Christianity, does not mean (or ought not mean) that an ideology of the insufficiency of history is not a widespread cultural reality and, we might add, possibility.

Niebuhr applies this idea with particular effectiveness in his criticisms of nationalistic messianism. This theme may have been rooted in his childhood experiences in an immigrant family. It certainly can be traced to a college course he took with the mentor of his youth, Samuel Press. The subject of that course was Amos, the Hebrew prophet who most sharply denounced ancient Israel's nationalism.[35] Press's instruction served Niebuhr well in later life. The critique of nationalism as a false prophetic voice came to the fore in the 1930s for the obvious reason of fascism's deadly evil. Though prompted by the immediate crisis of the late 1930s, Niebuhr's stern rebuke of false messianism seems also to have been behind his objections, first to liberalisms, then to Marxism, then generally to modernity's culture of inevitable progress itself. However it might be put, the general point is that variations on the theme of future progress that haunted the modern era were all too often calls for a false Christ—a state of anointment beyond the agonies of actual history.[36] In time, as the years passed into the 1940s, Niebuhr came to reserve an exacting censure for the American prophecy of its own special providence in the scheme of historical things.[37]

Nature and Destiny, not surprisingly, ends on a firmly Augustinian note: "It would be wrong to view the history of the world's many cultures and civilizations with an eye only upon their decline. They die in the end; but they also live. Their life is a testimony of the creativity of history, even as their death is a proof of the sin in history."[38] It is not by accident that Niebuhr returns to the theme of sin which had so focused the book as a whole—and return he did to the theory of sin that included a good many modern elements that were of the lineage of Augustine's *On the Trinity*.

If sin is taken as a distortion of the freedom and creativity of the human spirit, then sin cannot be simply a failure of the self, of the individual. The destiny of humanity—as a historical species—is bound up with humankind's natural incompleteness. No less collectively than individually, we are able to imagine so much more than we can know or do; hence we outrun ourselves. Pride overcomes humility. We begin to think of our nature as the true and final destiny of our species. We forget that we will die— as individuals, as communities, as civilizations, even as a species.

A planet of apes is not a joke. Any serious secular theory of the incompleteness of history would entail what the Greeks called an eschatology—a theory of the End of history. Modernity has so distorted the idea of "the End" into a utilitarian ideal of "the goal" that it has largely forgotten that it is human destiny to come to a true and final end. Cultures, as well as religions, may propose a definitive meaning beyond that End. Religious or not, individuals may take or leave them—ideally with the attitude of seriousness that such a prospect demands.

Augustine died in 430 in old age, four years after he finished *City of God*. When Niebuhr finished *Nature and Destiny of Man*, he was still in midlife. Even the stroke of 1952 did not end his productivity. As he recovered his ability to work, Niebuhr turned his attentions to the enduring subterranean effects of the crisis of the 1930s. No other book would match the genius of *Nature and Destiny*, but quite a few others would adumbrate its lessons. He would remain, ever after, Augustinian in his strong claims about the limits of human nature and destiny. "The wisdom about our destiny is dependent upon a humble recognition of the limits of our knowledge and our power."[39]

Niebuhr would never again write a book like *Nature and Destiny of Man*. It may have been that with this book he had laid down the groundwork on which he would stand. What he did thereafter was to engage global and domestic politics. The first of these political statements was *The Children of Light and the Children of Darkness: A Vindication of Democracy and a Critique of Its Traditional Defense*, which appeared in 1944 before the war was concluded. Some think of this book as a popularization of the themes developed in *Nature and Destiny*. It was, but only to the extent that nearly everything to follow could be traced back to his greatest work.

The Children of Light, however, was more an essay on the moral state of the world that the war still raging had already changed. In particular, it was, as its long subtitle announces, a well-thought-through but deeply felt attempt to assess the prospects of democracy. As usual, that assessment was double-edged: "Democracy, as every other historic ideal and institution, contains both ephemeral and more permanently valid elements. Democracy is on the one hand the characteristic fruit of a bourgeois civilization; on the other it is a permanently valuable form of social organization in which freedom and order are made to support, and not contradict, each other."[40] These words were written two years before the Cold War would follow the end of World War II. The book thereby does not address the question of communism directly. It was still fascism that occupied the world's moral conscience. For Niebuhr, the children of light thus were the "foolish" children of democracy—of, that is, the good that, however flawed, remained for global hope. The biblical figure of speech set the children of light against the children of darkness, who were evil. "For evil is always the assertion of some self-interest without regard for the whole, whether the whole be conceived as the immediate community, or the total community of mankind, or the total order of the world."[41] Shadows of Augustine's City of God against the City of Man are apparent. Yet also evident is the extent to which Niebuhr had already turned away from ancient history toward the history of times to come. If, in *Children of Light*, evil is the darkness of unbridled self-interest, then democracy with its roots in bourgeois civilization was at risk of giving up its permanent social values to the dark self-interests of the modern world. Fascism, in 1944, was still the foremost threat to democracy, but Niebuhr was able to see beyond the evil that was coming to its end to the future prospects of the postwar world, in which, he knew very well, democracy was at once its best hope and its own worst enemy.

As the global wars of the 1940s took their course, there came a time in the history of the modern West that was called the American Century—a journalist's facile slogan drawn upon the evidence that, as World War II progressed, only the United States could emerge as the supreme global power. Emerge it did, but its supremacy was short-lived. Within months of the conclusion of that war, the Cold War rose to take its place.

On their surface, the 1950s and early 1960s were times of relative abundance for the Americans and, in due course, of recovery and renewal in Europe and East Asia. But just below the surface, the deeper crisis of the modern West intruded upon the desire for prosperity. A culture founded on economic injustices going back to the early colonizing misadventures of Europe in the sixteenth century could not escape the crisis that was its destiny.

Thence followed the crisis that Niebuhr did not live to experience but was able to foresee—the fulfillment of the Augustinian insistence that all empires or, in modern times, nations will ultimately decline as they are forced to bow before the opposing forces of global reality.

It is not too difficult to imagine what Reinhold Niebuhr would say of political liberalism in twenty-first-century America, decades after his death. More sharply even than he rebuked the Social Gospel in the Detroit years, and, early in the New York years, than he resisted the liberal principles of Roosevelt's Democratic Party, Niebuhr would have been appalled by the ill-gotten compromises that, since 1980, have contributed to the destruction of the already fragile elements of a social welfare program in America. In both neoconservative and neoliberal compromises Niebuhr would have seen a failure of human pride—a failure ever more acute among liberals.[42] Conservatives, paradoxically, can be understood, if not forgiven, because, rhetoric aside, since the unraveling of Roosevelt's New Deal programs begun after 1968 under the perfectly evil Richard M. Nixon, American conservatives have, time and again, shown themselves bereft of any perceptible values other than those useful to the acquisition and holding of power. Liberals, however, by nature, do not trust power and thus lose it as soon as they gain it. Their opponents win it more often than they should because they, the conservatives, are willing to say and do anything that leads to power. Actual liberals, Niebuhr would surely say, are men (in his sense of the word), and thus just as capable of arrogance and evil as any other human being. But as political figures, their destiny is to yield to endlessly qualified reasons, to overconfidence in progress, to the illusion of the goodwill of the people.

What might Niebuhr have prescribed for a post-9/11 world? To unearth what in Niebuhr's thinking may be used in the current situation requires a political sensibility that, in effect, unlearns much of what modern culture has instilled in us—including pretty much everything about the inevitability of progress, the powers of the human individual, the direction of history as always forward and upward, and most of all the ready availability of the Good in this world. A political sensibility, thus cleansed, might be able to embrace Niebuhr's understanding of what sin is and is not; or, if the word *sin* is too strong for the queasy, instead of sin, we may come to understand those aspects of human nature that, whatever they are called, amount to the same thing.

Human nature is limited; human beings deny these limits; which denial leads them to believe too much in their own powers, too little in history as a series of steps forward and slips backward. In plain language, this is sin from which human society can escape only by recognizing that it cannot control history.

5

nations, global politics, and religion

irony and american history

As Niebuhr's discovery of Augustine in the 1930s allowed him to reclaim, you might say, the deep religious aspects of sin and the complexities of human nature, so the political realism that came from that rediscovery owed a considerable debt to what may have been his single most formative academic experience.

While still a youth at Eden College in Missouri, Niebuhr came upon a teacher who would shape him, personally and intellectually, for the rest of his days—shape him, perhaps, more even than the Detroit years and the Yale education. The person was Samuel D. Press, a teacher of extraordinary humanity and learning. Niebuhr came close to describing Press as a second father:

> The first formative influence on my life was my father, who combined a vital personal piety with a complete freedom in his theological studies. . . . I attended the college and seminary of my denomination. The little college had no more than junior college status in my day, and I was not interested in any academic disciplines. The seminary was influential in my life primarily because of the creative effect upon me of the life of a very remarkable man, Dr. S. D. Press, who combined a childlike innocency with a rigorous scholarship in Biblical and systematic subjects. This proved the point that an educational institution needs only to have Mark Hopkins on one end of a log and a student on the other.[1]

These lines are true witness to the hold Press had over (actually) both Niebuhr brothers.

For Reinhold, Press had a particular effect, one that fixed his life on prophetic work in both religion and politics. In particular, Press's teaching opened him to the complexities of international politics, and surely set his life course as a friend to Jewish people and ultimately to Israel—or, as one Jewish admirer felt, as a Jewish prophet in and of himself. For a young boy of German descent in the remote middle plains to have begun so many pilgrimages before maturity says a great deal about the boy, to be sure, but also about his teacher. Even great teachers do not anticipate the influence they have. And in the case of Press, it was far from clear that the teacher would have assigned quite as much importance to the one topic as it came to have in the pupil's life. The subject was Amos the great, first, and most aggressive of the ancient, eighth-century B.C.E. Hebrew prophets. Press's seminar at Eden College on Amos, along with his teachings on Paul, planted in Niebuhr the ideal of the prophetic preacher as a central theme in religious thought from Abraham through prophets like Amos and Ezekiel in the eighth and sixth centuries B.C.E. to Jesus, of course, through Paul and Augustine to the Protestant reformers.[2] It may well have been that Press's seminar on Amos so supplemented the influence of Reinhold's father as to shift his vocation from the pastoral to the prophetic ministry.

In either case, there is more to Amos than meets the eye. He is commonly considered a minor prophet. This because of the contrast with other, better-known, prophets. The Book of Isaiah (actually at least three sources in one) is the longer, more poetic, and more spiritually exalting of the prophetic books of the Jewish tradition. Jeremiah is a powerful poetic voice of the pain of Israel's failures. Others denounced Israel—Hosea, who castigated Israel as the whore unfaithful to its covenant with God, and Ezekiel, who dreamt of the dry bones of Israel reconstituting themselves after exile and defeat. Amos had many of the same qualities as these others, but he was distinctive for the way he balanced the two sides of the ancient prophet's message. Like Hosea, Amos is severe toward Israel: "For, lo [says the Lord], I will command, and I will sift the house of Israel among all nations, like as corn is sifted in a sieve, yet shall not the least grain fall upon the earth. All the sinners of my people shall die by the sword" (9:9–10). Yet in the next breath, like Ezekiel, even Isaiah, Amos renews God's promise to his people: "In that day will I raise up the tabernacle of David that is fallen, and close up the breaches thereof; and I will raise up his ruins, and I will build it as in the days of old" (9:11). Amos is among the great Hebrew prophets because he held together two opposing prophetic images—of severe condemnation and the promise of renewal, and thereby the prophet affirms his pastoral vocation.

Still, the subtlety of Amos's message to Israel is framed by the bluntness of his threats of destruction to the enemies of Israel—Damascus, Gaza, Edom, Moab, others, even Judah: "Thus sayeth the Lord; For three transgressions of Judah, and for four, I will not turn away the punishment thereof; because they have despised the law of the Lord, and have not kept his commandments, and their lies caused them to err" (2:4). In the end what puts Amos in a prophetic category of his own is that he strong-handedly denounces all the nations. For Isaiah, by contrast, Israel was a light to the nations, thus the source of historical redemption. For Amos all nations were unworthy of God's protection. Israel's hope was more remote than it was in other prophets, even in Ezekiel, even in Hosea.

In Amos's prophetic attitude we see intimations in Niebuhr's student days of the idea that emerged in *Moral Man and Immoral Society*—nations are unable to do the good that leads to justice for their people. And again, on a higher philosophical plane, the same idea, writ large, is in Niebuhr's concluding judgment on human destiny in this world: "Thus wisdom about our destiny is dependent upon a human recognition of the limits of our knowledge and power."[3]

Beyond this, there are two related hints of the importance of the Amos seminar at Eden College on Niebuhr's subsequent life. One is the extraordinary importance of Niebuhr's relations with and commitment to Jewish friends, notably Justice Felix Frankfurter, a summer companion in the Berkshires, and Rabbi Abraham Heschel, who said of Niebuhr after his death: "He appeared among us as a sublime figure out of the Hebrew Bible."[4] More generally, Niebuhr was a friend of Jewish people both during their suffering in Europe and in the founding of Israel and the assurance of its rights to the full status of a modern state.

As it happens, the long story of the struggle of the Hebrew people for nationhood—for their promised status as a nation among nations, as a "light to the nations," as Isaiah put it, referring to the gentiles—has been over the centuries unsettled. However tension-laden were the ancient beliefs about Israel's role in the scheme of worldly nations, the idea that some nations enjoy a special providence has endured into modern times. Most famously, the early American colonists conceived themselves and *their* new nation as on a mission to become the new Israel in the New World. Strictly speaking, the nation-state is a modern invention. Even so, the concept and the expression *nation* appeared commonly in the history of troubles of the Mesopotamian region in which the Jewish people were gathered out of many and various competing tribes. The so-called Cradle of Western Civilization was anything but a promised land of nurturing milk and honey. The region from the Euphrates in modern Iraq to the Nile in Egypt and the surrounding areas of the Eastern Mediterranean and the Arabian Desert—today known as the Middle East—was then as now a region of global conflict.

In biblical times, great global empires—the Persians, the Babylonians, the Greeks and Romans, the Ottomans, among others—dominated a conflict-torn region of smaller tribes and semi-independent peoples.[5] Nations, then, refer less to a formally ordered series of borders (as the Peace of Westphalia sought to achieve in 1648) than to constantly shifting centers of power dispersed along the crucial trade routes that linked East and West. Jerusalem today is the symbol of centuries of unsettled national and tribal interests. Called by many the world's most global city, Jerusalem represents the confluence of ethnic, religious, and political interests that have long put political order in the region and the world at risk. There is no lasting peace, but the failure of the nations comes from below—from the subterranean regions of enduring human conflict.

Today we speak of globalization. In Niebuhr's day no such word was available. Then, through his last days in the 1960s, the global realities were those organized by the Cold War—itself a remainder from a century of hot wars the world over. Thus, speaking again of Niebuhr's special relationship to the Hebrew prophets and to Jewish people, it is necessary at least to consider that for him the Jewish people were the true and original Diasporic peoples—the spiritual and cultural nomads who infused the world with learning and culture and by their firm prophetic claims engaged the world in struggles that among nations are never easily resolved. In a lecture in the 1950s to a joint meeting of the Union Theological and Jewish Theological seminaries in New York City, Niebuhr emphasized, among the exceptional qualities of Jewish culture, a "capacity for civil virtue."[6] In this respect, he believed, America and American Christians had much to learn from the Jews. Nations pursue interests, Niebuhr thought. Individual intentions cannot overcome national and social powers. In the balance hangs whatever can be done to find, make, and sustain what justice is possible.

The predicament remains as acute—and as open to solution—today as it did in the days of Niebuhr, Luther and Calvin, Augustine, Hosea and Amos, Abraham and the Hellenic city-state gods; and nowhere is it more acute than in America. On the secular side of the dilemma of human nature and destiny, no nation is more like what its early colonists wanted it to be—the new Israel. But as Niebuhr saw clearly, there is a profound irony in the claim of any nation, in any day, to be the light to the nations—to be, that is, the power able to make global things right. And this is where Niebuhr's least-known but most prescient book, *The Irony of American History*, comes in.

Niebuhr's America from 1915, when he began in Detroit, until his death in 1971 was a restless jumble. It still is. Most nations, especially those of Europe, draw on what came before to settle accounts with new realities. Europe, thus, having suffered destruction in World War II, rebuilt itself into a new democratic experiment that drew on the better angels of its past. America in 1945 took its international preeminence for granted. Europe took its first steps toward becoming what it is today—a postnational community of nations set on peace and prosperity at the price of stodginess.

Niebuhr would have appreciated Europe's commitment to a community of nations that put the question of a nation's independence in a new light. He thought that nations are first among the human communities that must contend with the issues of authority and domination: "All communities of mankind, from the most primordial, the family, to the large communities of nation and empire, are dependent on the one hand upon some internal force of cohesion and on the other hand upon the unifying power of a central authority."[7] Nationhood is achieved when the dilemma of cohesion and authority is resolved in a balanced way—just enough cohesion, not too much dominating authority. The balance point is seldom stable. When it comes to nationhood there may be many paths, but nations are relatively well settled only in two forms, determined by their histories. Nations that venerate their revolutionary origins are usually rabbit warrens of righteous confusions—the United States, Russia, China, Cuba. Nations that came into political being by fits and starts tend to be turtles—France, Brazil, the United Kingdom, India, Malaysia, and Indonesia, among others. Rabbits and turtles have their respective virtues and flaws, but they endure as nations. Otherwise, there are nations of fungible flag, unable or unwilling to settle the terms of their independent national nature—Congo, Mexico, Nigeria, Switzerland, the Koreas, Pakistan, Australia, Canada. Still others are more loose regional federations than nations—Mongolia, Nunavut, Rwanda, Barbary, Kashmir, Arabia, the Lakota, Oceania.

Nations are political territories claiming a conspicuous if not always operative cultural integrity. As national things go, staking a claim and defending a territory are relatively easy. Keeping a cohesive peace in the interior is much more difficult. Some say that multicultural conflict is both natural and healthy. Under the right circumstances this can be true. The problem is that in complicated worlds circumstances are seldom right enough to keep the conflict from soiling the civil sphere. Social and cultural differences interior to nations are messy, unruly, and therefore as toxic as state-sponsored exterior wars with other nations.

The idea and possibility of the modern nation-state is attributed to the Peace of Westphalia in 1648, when Spain, the Dutch, France, and other federations weary of more than a century of wars agreed, for the then time being, to respect territorial boundaries.[8] One could ask what makes for the distinction between a nation and an empire like Rome, or a phantom empire like, in 1648, the Holy Roman Empire. In the short run, very little, it seems. The Romans after Augustus, like the Dutch in the seventeenth century, were tightly bound by aqueducts and shipping lanes to their administrative centers. Both cast their territorial ambitions far beyond local hunting grounds.

At first, the difference between empires and nations appears to be overrated, except for one thing. As Immanuel Wallerstein has said in many places, the difference is that nation-states were from the start meant to be part of a global interstate system. The idea was to respect not just borders but governments that ruled in the name of a nation's traditions or laws. Interbreeding among royal families gave way in time to inherently fragile diplomatic accords. In principle, nations resort to war only when reason fails. The principle is often a way to buy time to work out a strategic exception. Yet the principle, however it may be used, serves a functional purpose, if not always a principled one. Neville Chamberlain was an ass, but his blunder at least exposed Hitler's imperial ambitions. The invasive war that followed served to resettle national boundaries around the world, thus allowing Europe, America, and East Asia to be what they have become.

Reinhold Niebuhr was, we have seen, prescient on this point. Nations move by perceived and arguable self-interests. They are little concerned with just and righteous rules, save when coerced. In a normal case, a nation finds its Dick Cheney, who reworks the rules in order to set loose the higher rule of ravenous economic interests. What safeguards Niebuhr's attitude from the charge of unqualified pessimism is, as in other things, his ironic view of history.

Large social institutions, like individual men and women, are capable of creativity even as they lapse into pride and selfishness. It may well be that the free individual is more consistently creative, but individuals can also be ferociously selfish. This is the enigma that neither Niebuhr nor anyone since has resolved particularly well. Individuals act more or less autonomously— sometimes well, sometimes poorly. Yet as hard as it may be to detect what individuals intend by their actions, by contrast the historical record of very large social structures is a blinding swarm of bees. Reports on the behavior of states and nations are at best synecdochical. *The White House said. The Kremlin protested. The Nikkei fell.* Below the skin of broadcast news and the skeletal archives, historical events are buried in a cavernous emptiness. Given the magnitudes of state power, not to mention the modern state's technologies of deception, what we cannot know of collective motives is colossal compared with what we will not or cannot understand about the inner workings of the individual.

Niebuhr was a bit off when he spoke of the selfishness of societies, as if states and other social structures had motives or intentions of the same order as those of individuals. In the long run, he recoiled from the simplicity of his early statements.[9] Still, as clear as he was on the basic issue, the false ascription of moral intentions (as distinct from actions) to states (among other collectivities) has resisted Niebuhr's wisdom. In fact, his thinking on this score may be less well accepted in a day like ours, when media streaming of ill-formed opinions dominates political chat. At issue is not the nastiness of political talk radio and its affines. Politicians and their advocates have always spoken ill of each other. The great problem, Niebuhr thought, was the naïve assumption that individual ethics apply to societies. Thus today, when media encourage immediate and total access to the public and private lives of public figures, anyone with a keyboard can be an amateur psychoanalyst of interior intentions. You seldom hear serious analysis of what public figures say and do, which would be the analysis of the role of their positions in a society's structures. Presidents and prime ministers do terrible things. They lie, they tell half-truths, they command murderous wars, they apply pressure to recalcitrants, and so forth. Hence the legitimation crisis of democratic societies that Jürgen Habermas (following Max Weber) so well identified years ago.[10]

Democracies face an inevitable dilemma. States are meant to obey "the people" and to govern in their name. But the people organize themselves into conflicting groups sympathetic to their grievances and insensitive to those of other groups. Conflict ensues. In the face of the inevitable, those who govern have only two choices. Either lie and hope it all works out, or tell the full truth to an already suspicious public. Either way truth does not out. Cable and radio talk aggravates the public figure's impossible situation. Some survive with their better reputations intact, but seldom without a moment or two of trouble. FDR was a cripple; JFK a womanizer; RMN was at least a drunk. FDR's disability, they overlooked. JFK's womanizing, they ignored. RMN they disgraced, but not for the drinking. Most got by until they could not. They were real individuals with real human failings. Even the worst work to some good—ending a war, avoiding a nuclear holocaust, opening China. They held great power over the destiny of nations and had to hold it in spite of their human incapacities, in respect to which they wanted to control what was known about their true interior selves. In this the high and mighty are little different from the pimply teenage boy who wants to cover the nerdish truth of his ill-formed being.

Niebuhr understood the problem well. In his books and speeches after 1952, with uncanny fairness he addressed the nuances of the individuals who were responsible for the administration of nations. He thought it a not a bad thing that in 1952 Dwight Eisenhower, of whom Niebuhr did not wholly disapprove, defeated Adlai Stevenson, whom he suppported.[11] This, he said, because it is never a good thing for one party (in this case the Democrats) to hold all the power (the White House and the Congress) or to hold administrative power too long (from Roosevelt in 1933 to Truman in 1953). The election of Eisenhower meant also that the business and corporate interests of the Republication Party bore responsibility for policy, forcing the conservative wing of the party into the background. Likewise, after Nikita Khrushchev's 1959 visit to the United States, Niebuhr was far from seduced by the Soviet leader's convivial public style. He soberly thought Khrushchev, in spite of his liberalization policies, was not that much different from Stalin. The Soviet system, like the American one, was a system. Individual politicians can tweak the details but not the structures.[12]

Niebuhr was at his best when contrasting individuals to the social structures they encounter. From *Moral Man and Immoral Society* (1932) through his long Augustinian awakening culminating in *Nature and Destiny of Man* (1941–43), Niebuhr challenged his readers to confront the social limitations of the ethical individual. The books after his stroke in 1952 included works that revised and played out the themes of earlier writing: *The Self and the Dramas of History* (1955) and *Man's Nature and His Communities: Essays on the Dynamics and Enigmas of Man's Personal and Social Existence* (1965). Yet the most striking subject to emerge in this period was the fate of democracy and, in particular, of American democracy: *Christian Realism and Political Problems* (1953), *The World Crisis and American Responsibility* (1958), and *The Democratic Experience* (1969). Even *The Structure of Nations and Empires: A Study of the Recurring Patterns and Problems of the Political Order in Relation to the Unique Problems of the Nuclear Age* (1959), its cumbersome subtitle notwithstanding, was largely preoccupied with the fate of the American democratic state, as was the earliest and best of the political theories of period, *The Irony of American History* (1952), which was based on lectures given in 1949 and 1951, before the stroke.

But how can anyone of even vaguely left commitments recommend Niebuhr's ideas, given that in the last years of life he was such a Cold Warrior?[13] The moniker may be too strong when Niebuhr is compared with mindless ideologues like Joseph McCarthy, whom he denounced in 1953, well before others had. But it is true that Niebuhr also denounced not only Soviet Communism but communisms of all brands. How could a thinker on the left, whatever the political realities of his time, assume a public position that, in our day, seems so obnoxious?

Ultimately, the answer turns on what is made of the history of the Cold War from, say, 1945 at Yalta and the trouble it made in the Velvet Revolution of 1989 and its sequelae. Two opposite if not utterly different outlooks came to dominate. From the more generous vantage, the Cold War was a stupid, wasteful, and deadly struggle that made a mockery of the sacrifices of those who died in World War II. To the degree that the defeat of fascism and imperialism in 1945 was intended to preserve democracies and human freedoms, the Cold War was a perversion at best and a travesty at worst. The opposing and less forgiving view was that Soviet and Maoist communisms were a real threat to those democracies—a threat demonstrated by Stalin's Gulag and Mao's Cultural Revolution, in which untold millions lost their lives—more, some think, than the millions lost to Hitler's Holocaust. The former, somewhat liberal, position is that bad things happen as a consequence of human foolishness. The later, more conservative, interpretation is that what happened was not merely bad but a civilization threatening evil.

Niebuhr always put himself in the betweens of history. There was, he thought, no pure political truth among ideologies that derive from abstract ideals and move toward perfectionist outcomes. His Augustinian interpretation of history in *Nature and Destiny* was, in this respect, a mature version of his critique of American liberalisms of all kinds and of all Marxisms. His subtle interpretation of history as eschatological-but-not-utopian demanded that he reject all theories of human destiny that fail to recognize that the End of history is, if not near at hand, an ever-always possibility.

This is a realism that chastens all political judgments. Niebuhr's realism was decidedly not Realpolitik in the late-modern Strangelovian tradition of Kissinger, Cheney, and Rumsfeld. Enemies are real, they say; and must thereby be realistically attacked by any means necessary. One negotiates, if at all, only when (as in Kissinger's settlement with Hanoi) superiority is insufficient to domination. This is the realism of present dangers understood from the standpoint of an absolutistic theory of historical progress. This sort of realism works occasionally in the short run until it runs into longer, complicated historical realities that call out the impossibility that any one actual political history could be the universal answer to humankind's destiny. Marxism is liberalism in wolf's clothing. Both leave their proponents at the risk of being eaten alive by their naïveté.

By contrast, Niebuhr's Christian and political realism was of another kind. The end of history was for him not a *terminus ad quem*, a point toward which a temporal vector inexorably moved. His idea of the End, like Augustine's, was more the hazard that at any given moment the course of history could be interrupted. Political realism of Niebuhr's kind falls under the crude rubric Shit Happens! It is not that human history is diarrheic, but that whatever may be good is not the final word. Wheat and weeds cannot be separated until the One who sows harvests. To be sure, Niebuhr's eschatology, his theory of the limitations of history, was derived from his evangelical Christianity. The ideals of a perfectible progress toward pure market freedoms or of a class-less utopia simply do not allow for a messianic interruption. Not even Marx's theory that the contradictions of capitalism will eventually assert themselves to the effect of a revolution ending the exploitative rule of the bourgeois class qualifies as historically honest realism. The key idea is in the *eventuality* which is taken as a necessity. It *will* happen even if we don't know exactly when. A god of a people who believe in history is vastly more likely to chasten them against their pride than is any modern ideology. The reproach of pride is the beginning of realism.

Those few who have been (or have tried to be) political realists in Niebuhr's sense know, as he knew, that the realist's attitude toward participation in history must begin with humility. Humility alone is not sufficient to political thought and work, but it is where the realist begins. This is not an entirely strange idea in ordinary human consciousness. In fact, we know that we never know—when a tower will crash, an assassin will strike, the waters will flood, a heart will attack itself. When it is said that a person died of "natural causes," what is meant is that no one knows why, exactly, he was struck down then and there. A sudden crisis in the night is the most natural cause of history's turns. Death is the answer to life—the ending that quickens the remaining days that will wither and be cut down. Actual human history is less a series of life-giving events than the creative acceptance of the conclusive end under which all things human subsist. To accept the morbidity of liveliness is not pessimism. It is, in a word, the realism that mocks our innocent optimisms.

What, then, was the reality of the Cold War so far as Niebuhr was concerned? First, though he was through and through what today what we might call a globalist, it is impossible to understand Niebuhr's politics apart from his critical appreciation of American history and politics. Niebuhr stands out among social critics because he had become, as had his father, so deeply American. He had learned to accept democracy as an interior aptitude before it was an ideological program. What so moved Reinhold as a boy, when his father was sincerely interested in his opinion, was Gustav's abiding democratic soul—a soul that moved the son through life.

Listen to any of the recordings of Reinhold's lectures at Union, his speeches, or his radio talks, and you will hear that spirit. In an ABC radio program broadcast in 1960, for one example, he was scheduled to discuss "Communism and Christianity." Joining him was an aggressively cautious academic—an expert in Soviet studies who had lived in the Soviet Union for some time and taught Russian area studies at a distinguished university. The conversation was formal and high-minded. The expert was stuffily arrogant, unable to give more than a short inch to Niebuhr's views while more than willing to stipulate his superior knowledge not only of communism but of Christianity.[14]

Niebuhr was unfailingly generous and respectful. Naturally, at every turn the expert was distrustful of the Soviet regime and hostile to communist ideology. As was then the norm among academics and foreign affairs specialists, he worked from the assumption that the American alternative was "Christian" and thereby superior. Niebuhr ceded what he could, but in an authoritative yet kindly way he insisted that neither was superior to the other and that both the United States and the USSR were corrupt.[15] Both were nationalistic civil religions that had lost their souls.[16] Niebuhr was on nationwide radio so he did not press the finer points of his theory of history, yet they were there to be heard. Listening to the recording exposes the decency of Niebuhr's manner and the delicacy of his thought. One readily understands the interior force of his realism. Niebuhr had the uncommon gift of being able, without the wild talk and the dancing about, of stinging like a bee while floating like a butterfly. The patience was an aspect of Niebuhr's personal humility that led to his political realism. Those with their eyes set on the gods can afford to be less anxious about the immediate situation.

In the 1950s the political situation in America was crimped on all sides by the Cold War and the damage it was doing to America's collective mind. The Cold War began early in 1946—less than a year after World War II ended. The seeds of it were of course already evident in Stalin's behavior at Yalta. The U.S.-USSR rivalry developed soon after into a full-blown American dread of communism; then came Mao's defeat of the Nationalists (1949), the Korean War (1950–53), the American intervention in Vietnam upon the failure of the French (1954), the recognition that the Soviets had in some areas surpassed the United States technologically (Sputnik, 1957), the Berlin Wall (1960), and the failed invasion of Cuba (1961). The Cuban missile crisis (1962) could not have been imagined in 1945. President Kennedy's opening challenge to the Soviets in the 1962 crisis: "It shall be the policy of this nation to regard any nuclear missile launched from Cuba against any nation in the Western Hemisphere as an attack on the United States, requiring a full retaliatory response upon the Soviet Union." Such a prospect was terrifying for those who lived through those days, but it was merely the worst case of a dangerous game already well in play.

Niebuhr was indeed a Cold Warrior in the sense that he understood the dire straits into which the world had fallen and agreed that the communist menace was at the heart of the problem. But he did not excuse America from its role in this sordid business. Niebuhr was not an ideological nationalist. He was a patriot who understood that the Russian heritage of the Soviet regime lent the Russians a legitimate, if (as in the United States) troubled, patriotism. Insofar as patriotism is a nationalistic sentiment, this was damning with faint praise. Niebuhr's early idea that societies are by their nature immoral was never as fitting as during the Cold War. Two military and technological giants, each with its own justifiably robust cultural traditions, emerged from the good they did in Europe in defeating Hitler to take on the mantle of their worst nationalistic premises.

Economically, the Americans had the upper hand throughout the Cold War and thus had every reason to relax in their triumph in the war of the 1940s and the stupendous industrial productivity they had developed in the fight against Japan and Germany. By 1950 the United States produced more than half the world's industrial output.[17] The Soviets were still industrial adolescents when the Union collapsed in 1991. Its manufacturing sector had been overwhelmingly directed at military and technological ends. In this respect, you could say (though in the 1950s no one but Niebuhr and a few others dared to) that the Soviets had more reason to distrust the Americans than the reverse. They knew how comparatively weak their economy was. Like the teenage gangster, they affected bravado to cover the inferiority complex.

It is thus not surprising that Joseph Stalin's opening salvo in the Cold War, on February 9, 1946, was framed as a structural critique of capitalism and unqualified praise of the Soviet system:

> Marxists declare that the capitalist system of world economy conceals elements of crisis and war, that the development of world capitalism does not follow a steady and even course forward, but proceeds through crises and catastrophes. The uneven development of the capitalist countries leads in time to sharp disturbances in their relations. . . . Perhaps the catastrophe of [the Second World War] could have been avoided if the possibility of periodic redistribution of raw materials and markets between the countries existed in accordance with their economic needs, in the way of coordinated and peaceful decisions. But this is impossible under the present capitalist development of world economy. . . . As far as our country is concerned, [World War II] was the most cruel and hard of all wars ever experienced in the history of our motherland. But the war has not only been a curse; it was at the same time a hard school of trial and a testing of all the people's forces. . . . Now victory means, first of all,

that our Soviet social system has won, that the Soviet social system has successfully stood the test in the fire of war and has proved its complete vitality. . . . The war has shown that the Soviet multi-national state system has successfully stood the test, has grown still stronger during the war and has proved a completely vital state system.[18]

Stalin, like the Soviet leaders that followed him, affirmed the "spirit" of their system, rattled their sabers, exhibited their technological advances, but they could not disguise the failure of the Soviet system to compete across the full range of economic productivity.

Thirteen years later, on July 24, 1959, just weeks before Nikita Khrushchev visited the United States at the end of September, he met the American vice president, Richard Nixon, in Moscow at an exhibition of American kitchen conveniences. This was the occasion of the silly but famous "kitchen debate." Nixon and Khrushchev argued the relative virtues of their two systems. Nixon bragged of the brilliance of American consumer products. Khrushchev countered Nixon with the Soviet system's promise of economic justice: "In Russia, all you have to do to get a house is to be born in the Soviet Union. You are entitled to housing. . . . In America, if you don't have a dollar you have a right to choose between sleeping in a house or on the pavement. Yet you say we are the slave to Communism." Thirty-plus years after the kitchen debate, in 1991, the Soviet Union ended, in large part because it was unable to wage war or threaten war while also providing the freely evident consumption goods available in the West.

Meanwhile, one can fairly wonder why exactly the Americans engaged the Cold War so vehemently, and on what basis. Niebuhr's answer was clear, and clearly determined by his political realism. He wrote in 1959:

> The modern world is divided by two opposing alliances of nations. Each is under the hegemony of a nation which has the economic and military strength to determine independent policy. . . . The Russian leadership is more obviously ideological because it is, according to the unifying dogma, the "fatherland" of Communism and is destined to come to the support of any communist country. Our hegemony is not as consistently ideological because the noncommunist nations include not only the western democracies but many nations of East and West who are not communist. Among the western nations there would be few who would regard us as the perfect exemplars of the democratic creed. We are merely the strongest of these nations.[19]

Niebuhr gave not a jot to the pervasively limiting effects of America's ideological liberalism.

Niebuhr's objection to liberal individualisms that underplayed the role of community and society in the formation of a moral self did not cause him to dismiss the importance of what he called the biblical (which is to say Augustinian) idea of the historical self:

> The engagement of sensitive individuals or for that matter of any individuals, in the perplexities and perils of nations, cultures, and even of the whole enterprise of civilization . . . does not annul any private hopes or ambitions or simplify the drama of any individual life. Our contemporary situation [1955, at the height of the Cold War] is a vivid reminder of the fact that while history constantly enlarges the scope of the collective drama which becomes the basis

of all individual destinies, it does not obviate any of the problems the single self faces in its involvement in, and transcendence over, its collective destinies.[20]

Niebuhr was, if not a Cold Warrior, opposed to communism for reasons similar to those that had led to his criticism of liberalism.[21] The one, communism, had little place for the dramas of the individual; the other, liberalism, was ignorant of the necessity of collective association. Both stood on principles they undermined. Communism affirmed, in a distorted way, the principle of social justice. Liberalism distorted the rights and freedoms of the individual. Niebuhr's philosophical scalpel exposed both sides of the American Cold War in the 1950s.

Abroad, the only truly hot moment in the Cold War was in Korea from 1950 to 1953 (four years almost to the day), when the American-led United Nations police action fought Communist North Korea and China. The Communists nearly pushed the U.N. forces off the peninsula until General Douglas MacArthur's end run by sea to Inchon cut the North off from its supply lines from China. The world was then on the verge of a nuclear disaster prevented only when President Truman put an end to MacArthur's command and to his ambition for a wider war with China. Back home in the United States, in nearly the same period (and not unrelated to the Korean War), Senator Joseph McCarthy conducted a political and social reign of terror from 1950 until his censure in 1954. The precipitating crisis of both the Korean War and the Red Scare was the Communist defeat of the pro-American Nationalists in China in 1949. The Cold War with the Russians, by then well into its fourth year, had at least the historical value of having begun in 1917 with the overturning of the feudal order of the Russian czars. But in China, the Nationalists emerged from the modernizing party that in 1912 had overthrown the Qing, the last of China's ancient dynasties. That in 1949 the Communists would defeat the U.S.-supported Nationalists was a revolting development to the universal ideology of Western culture. To the Americans, Mao's victory was not only Communist but, in the racist ignorance of that day, inscrutably Asian.[22] Mao took power in 1949. This was but five years after the end of the long war against Japan and only another five to come before America would involve itself in Vietnam after the French defeat in 1954.

From 1946 to the Korean War in 1950 and the early participation in Vietnam in 1954 to the bizarre rejection of Castro's Cuban Revolution in 1959, the United States followed its ideological nose to pursue a Cold War foreign policy that at its end in 1991 left little to show for the pain and suffering. Communism had fallen, to be sure, but had it been the menace Americans had come to believe it was? Have there not been, since, ideological enemies just as menacing as either the Soviets or the Maoists? Strategically, there will probably never be a final resolution of the debate over the true nature of communist menace. Neither the Soviets nor the Chinese were benign. But were they so real a threat as to justify America's diplomatic and military foolishness? It is hard even to discern who started the whole thing.

What is clear is that in 1946 the Americans started off on the wrong foot. Just thirteen days after Stalin's 1946 election speech proclaiming Russia's geopolitical virtue, the American diplomat

George Kennan sent Moscow the long State Department tele-gram that laid out the principles of and justification for America's national interest in the containment of communism. Kennan was educated at Princeton. He was cultured and smart where Joseph McCarthy was neither. Still, it is remarkable that what may be the most influential secret document of the twentieth century was composed, in part, as an amateurish psychology of Russian and Soviet collective psychology:

> At bottom of Kremlin's neurotic view of world affairs is traditional and instinctive Russian sense of insecurity. Originally, this was inse-curity of a peaceful agricultural people trying to live on vast exposed plain in neighborhood of fierce nomadic peoples. To this was added, as Russia came into contact with economically advanced West, fear of more competent, more powerful, more highly organized societies in that area. But this latter type of insecurity was one which afflicted rather Russian rulers than Russian people; for Russian rulers have invariably sensed that their rule was relatively archaic in form, fragile and artificial in its psychological foundation, unable to stand comparison or contact with political systems of Western countries. For this reason they have always feared foreign penetration, feared direct contact between Western world and their own, feared what would happen if Russians learned truth about world without or if foreigners learned truth about world within. And they have learned to seek security only in patient but deadly struggle for total destruc-tion of rival power, never in compacts and compromises with it.[23]

There could hardly be a more fateful example of Niebuhr's idea that liberal individualism mixed with nationalistic fervor is as dangerous in its way as are collectivist nationalist ideologies. When state interests permeate the morality of societies and nations, little room is left for just reasoning.

What Kennan thought was that the isolation of the Russian people led them to Marxism. "It was no coincidence," he argued, "that Marxism, which had smoldered ineffectively for half a century in Western Europe, caught hold and blazed for [the] first time in Russia." This left the Soviets, he thought, with no options beyond "patient but deadly struggle for the destruction of a rival power." Kennan's rhetoric was cool, his logic hot. This was February 1946, nine months after the unconditional surrender of the Nazis to the Allies and Russia and two weeks before Winston Churchill popularized the logic of a Soviet Iron Curtain.

Nor was it a coincidence that within a few years in the United States there was already brewing a concern that America, so soon after an astonishing war victory, was losing its moral edge. In 1950 David Riesman's *The Lonely Crowd*, written with two other University of Chicago sociologists, was the first of number of serious books arguing, in effect, a decline in American culture. Riesman's idea was that postwar affluence was turning America from an inner-directed nation of productive individuals into an other-directed culture of consuming conformists. Also in 1950 the psychoanalyst Erik Erikson would coin the term *identity crisis*, which, with *lonely crowd*, would become a popular catch-phrase for the times. Over the decade of the 1950s other expressions came into currency, coined by well-regarded intellectuals: *the affluent society* (John Kenneth Galbraith), *the organization man* (William H. White), *impression management* (Erving Goffman); and these were the high-culture social critics. Countless other mass-culture books and essays converged on the theme of America's lost individualism.

Apart from America's anticommunist obsession, something else was going in the culture. In the political arena, the Red Scare may well have been a mass-culture analogue to the high-culture debate over national character. The lowbrow attitude simply stipulated the superiority of America's moral character; the high-brows were filled with regret that it was in decline. Reinhold Niebuhr, again, had the clearer idea—an idea that applies as well today as would have in the 1950s, had it been taken to heart:

> Our foreign policy reveals even more marked contradictions between our early illusions of innocency and the hard realities of the present day than do our domestic policies. We lived for a century not only in the illusion but in the reality of our innocency in our foreign relations. We lacked the power in the first instance to become involved in the guilt of its use. As we gradually achieved power, through the economic consequences of our richly stored continent, the continental unity of our economy and the technical efficiency of our business and industrial enterprise, we sought for a time to preserve innocency by disavowing the responsibilities of power.[24]

What was presented as principle in the Cold War turned out to be a naïve failure to come to terms with America's newfound position in the world after World War II. Kennan accused the Russians of being unable to enter into reasoned compacts, a complaint that downplayed the USSR's ability to engage the United States in a deadly struggle for world dominance. In 1945 America was truly dominant in every important social and economic sense. Beginning the year following, the United States led the West back to the too simple principles of individualism in a world that was no longer as it had been in the nineteenth century—and no longer that because the United States was not just the new global power but a different kind of power among the nations—a power constrained by a culture of moral individualism that proved inept for its global interests.

Sooner or later, principles applied to global politics create double binds. Power permeates the abyss between the ideal and the realities. Thus where principles are set so high above ordinary realities, as they are in America, power will always be an unsettled subject. The idea in modern liberal cultures is that political actions informed by good ideas can be reasonable. In reality they seldom are, any more than informing values can be purebred. Power is thus the agony of all liberal judgments—legal, personal, religious, social, racial, economic. In cultures like the American one, where normal, necessary social discriminations are considered wrong, principle runs up against the realities of power, leading the politicians and other false prophets of the ideal to make inequalities appear as if they were an illusion.

Why in America did individualism become so prominent? Both individualism itself and the social criticism of its effects were the exclusive ideological properties of the Americans who in the seventeenth century learned them from the British and the French. The very term *individualism* was coined by a Frenchman, Alexis de Tocqueville.[25] But he invented the expression to characterize what he had observed during his travels in the United States in the 1830s. Niebuhr quotes Tocqueville in *American Democracy* in 1835 to the effect of individualism on the spiritual pride of the Americans:

The illusions of innocence were not confined to our earliest years. De Tocqueville was made aware of them again and again on the American Frontier: "If I say to an American," he reported, "that the country is a fine one, aye he replies and there is not its equal in the world." If I applaud the freedom its inhabitants enjoy, he answers "freedom is a fine thing but few nations are worthy of it." If I remark on the purity of the morals that distinguishes the United States he declares "I can imagine that a stranger who has witnessed the corruption which prevails in other nations would be astonished at the difference." At length I leave him to a contemplation of himself.[26]

When individualism is the fundamental shared virtue, then a nation comprising so many individualists will exaggerate the normal pride of the patriot. Tocqueville, who was generally sympathetic to the American cause, concludes the passage Niebuhr quotes: "It is impossible to conceive of a more troublesome and garrulous patriotism."

There are many attempts to explain American individualism and how it transposed itself into an extreme form of political liberalism. But the account that best conveys Niebuhr's appreciation of the problem is that individualism as it came to be in American life is a disposition native to the Protestant mind. No place on earth better embodies the dilemmas and possibilities of the Protestant principle and all that comes with it.

Of the 600 million Protestants the world over, nearly a third (roughly 180 million) are in North America—more by far than in any other large global region on the planet. In the United States alone there are 160 million, roughly 55 percent of the population. No other country has more than a fifth of that number (the United Kingdom has 36 million, but this includes mostly Anglicans, a faux Protestant sect); and those few that have a higher percentage have small populations (like Denmark, with 91 percent but gathered in an official state religion to which almost no one pays attention).[27] In the United States, though Catholicism is the largest single denomination (approximately 72 million in 2005), the influence of the twice as many affiliated with Protestant groups is indicated by the degree to which members of the Roman Church live according to values that conform more closely to the prevailing values of the country as a whole—especially and obviously on matters of sexual practices and abortion rights.[28] The key is less in the numbers than in the influence of protestantizing ideas on the national culture; hence the omnipresence of essentially Protestant ideas in American public life and culture.

When politicians and other public figures, including preachers, refer to America as a Christian nation, they are speaking a cultural truth that reflects the historic importance of Protestantism. This is an effect that, again, is explained by the widely accepted thesis of Max Weber. In *The Protestant Ethic and the Spirit of Capitalism*, Weber argued that sixteenth-century Reformed Protestantism gave the modern world an ethical orientation to rational conduct in everyday life—a value that is severely focused on the individual as the moral agent of economic and social enterprise. Individualism in the form of a uniquely American adaptation of the rights of the individual had its roots in Calvinism in the sixteenth century—if, that is, Max Weber was correct. On the surface, there is a huge difference between the stern moral individualism of the early Puritan divines in the New England colonies and the rapacious corporate entrepreneurs of industrial capitalism. Yet apart from the degrees of moral separation, the types of individual, separated by centuries in time, share an essentially utilitarian ethic. Each believes that the means to the end—of salvation by grace alone or of self-fulfillment by profit—is found in living a life of disciplined, calculating, future-directed hard work. This is what Weber called "this-worldly asceticism"—a remarkably pliable phrase that allowed him to link, over time, an originally religious principle with the thoroughly secular values of the capitalist entrepreneur. In *The Protestant Ethic and the Spirit of Capitalism*, when all of the historical details are boiled down to their essence, Weber argued, there is no difference in ethical behavior between the Puritan divine who reviewed the attendance records on the Sabbath in order to fix the week's strategic plan for correcting the morally wayward and the factory owner who reviews the balance sheets to calculate the means to his best profit margins. Each has a calculus by which he determines the value of his individual worth, thereby to maximize economic or spiritual profits.

Like Protestantism itself, and largely because of it, America is where this kind of calculating individualism is rampant. It is found elsewhere, but only in America is it so much the order of the day. When Americans think of freedom, they think of the freedom of the individual from constraints of all kinds, whether the noise of their undesirable neighbors or the perceived intrusions of their government. This is not, to be sure, the sum and substance of the Protestant ethic (or of American politics). But it is more than fair to say that this is how the Protestant principle has played out historically in America.

And this, too, is why the American attitude toward power is both distinctive and derivative of the nation's cultural history. The classic definition of power is notoriously that of Thrasymachus in fifth-century Greece: justice is the power of the strong. But—and again, it was Max Weber who put it in analytic and modern terms—power is the ability of A to force B to act against his will, where the A and the B can be groups or classes, as well as individuals.[29] Until innovations like those of Michel Foucault, power almost exclusively was seen as domination—as, thus, the enemy of fairness and justice, accordingly, the evil force against which human rights are meant to protect. In one version the individual protects himself best by ceding authority to state power. This is the line that began with Thomas Hobbes. The other version is that associated with Adam Smith and the wider utilitarian philosophy which thinks that the individual does best when left to his enlightened self-interests. Either way, modern ideas of individualism are associated with a uniquely modern antipathy to power as a positive force in human affairs. You can find variants of this suspicion of power's trouble everywhere in the European Diaspora where Enlightenment values have spread. But, and still again, nowhere is it more pronounced, even exaggerated, than in the United States.

One of the reasons America has had no political left in the European sense of organized parties favoring a quasi-socialist welfare program is its deeper hostility to state power. This, too, is why America's peculiarly tepid liberal-left traditions have faltered before conservative aggressions and why, thereby, the United States has enjoyed only one very short period in which the federal government was managed as a strong state system commanding social forces to fight economic misery at home and evil abroad. It took the double-barreled threats of Depression and Fascism in the 1930s to elect and reelect FDR, a political genius able and willing to manage American affairs with full and honest appreciation of political power—defined, that is, as the willingness of the A's to provide for the safety and needs of B's. The only other time when anything similar occurred was when Abraham Lincoln defied the Confederacy by mobilizing the North to defend the social Union. You might possibly include Teddy Roosevelt's defiance of the corporate interests of his day. But neither Lincoln nor the Roosevelts were anything like European Socialists.

In America, an unambiguous, if not seriously radical, Left prevailed only in the short period of FDR's administrations and episodically thereafter until the election of Richard Nixon in 1968. Thirty-six years, plus or minus, from 1932 to 1968, is but a fraction of the nation's political history—a history that began in settlement of the original colonies by individualizing religious groups escaping Europe's social oppressions as they saw it; then continued in a revolution which led to a political system devoted admirably and significantly to the balance of powers—a kind of weak acknowledgment that a modern state must use its power, especially in foreign relations, but that structurally those powers must be checked. But also a principle convenient to the values of founding fathers who were flawed gentry with yeoman convictions. Jefferson, Adams, and Madison were the pure types, but the variants were notable for their similarity. Even Benjamin Franklin, who began as a commercial printer and found favor in British and French high societies, morphed into a version of what Crevecoeur in *Letters from an American Farmer* (1784) called "this new man," the American individual.

The allegedly new individualism is, without question, the motive force behind whatever is creative in American history, as it is behind the evil that America, like other nations of prideful power, has wrought. Characteristically, Niebuhr put the point in more high-minded terms than history tells:

> The prosperity of America is legendary. Our standards of living are beyond the dreams of avarice of most the world. We are a kind of paradise of domestic security and wealth. But we face the ironic situation that the same technical efficiency which provided our comforts has also placed us at the center of the technical developments in world events. There are evidently limits to the achievements of science; and there are irresolvable contradictions both between the prosperity and virtue, and between happiness and the "good life" which had not been anticipated in our philosophy. The discovery of these contradictions threatens our culture with despair.[30]

Niebuhr in 1952 shared the gathering concern among intellectuals like David Riesman, who felt America was losing its moral edge. But Niebuhr, as always, came up short of analyzing it as if histories, including the American one, could be plotted along a straight-line trajectory that moves ever upward—until, that is, it dips toward despair. Niebuhr thought in terms of contradictions. The threat of despair was real only because, in his word, the American "philosophy" had no sense of the irony of its history, of all histories.

By 1959 Niebuhr would harden his line on the American philosophy as it faltered in the decade after World War II, when the United States, having risen to the status of a global hegemonic power, was in effect cowed by the Soviet challenge *and* naïve with respect to the realities of its global responsibilities:

> One must draw the conclusion that some deep stream in American life and thought is responsible for reactions which are so at variance with the realities. This stream of liberal democratic theory of foreign relations is wider and deeper than American thought and life. . . . [Still] the liberal democratic theory seems to have two emphases: (1) an emphasis on the integrity and autonomy of the nation, and (2) a vague universalism or consideration of the "community of mankind" which leaves little room for the configurations of power and authority which develop in history between the nation and the university community.[31]

If the liberal nations of the North Atlantic were philosophically ill-equipped to face the realities of the Soviet hegemon, then the responsibility lay overwhelmingly with the Americans, who, after all, held the lion's share of economic and military power.

Yet as subsequent history would reveal, exceptions being noted, Europe would emerge from its period of postwar reconstruction vastly less liberal in Niebuhr's class sense and less willing (or able) to exercise global power. Europe's twentieth century, beginning with the war of 1914, was longer already than

America's, as its intellectual and cultural resources ran deeper. As time would tell in the years after Niebuhr's warnings had been ignored, America's political philosophy would continue to drift on the surface of an essentially discredited economic and political ideology. Its misadventures, from Vietnam through Somalia to Iraq and Afghanistan, made the Korean War appear downright honest.

Needless to say, America's religious enthusiasms have been unusual among modern industrial nations. The staying power of organized religion in America confounds the experts, who, since early in the industrial era in the mid-nineteenth century, assumed or predicted that as the modern secular business ethic advanced, religion would decline. Even Max Weber agreed in rough terms with Marx, Freud, and Durkheim that religion would eventually fade from the urbanized landscape. In Europe it has, but not in the United States.

Niebuhr believed America's exceptional religiosity grew out of its messianic faith in itself—a faith he had described in *Nature and Destiny of Man*: "On the egoistic-nationalistic level Messianism looks forward to the triumph of the nation, empire or culture in which the Messianic hope is expressed."[32] Nationalistic messianism, thus understood, denies the realities of history. Nationalisms are themselves distortions of the historical facts. When they escalate into a messianic doctrine, enthusiasm for the national ideals become something still more dangerous. As Tocqueville discovered in the 1830s, American patriotism can be extreme. Perhaps one might excuse the excesses when found among a people so new to the community of nations. There are occasions when what Niebuhr called the innocence of a young nation combines with an unusually rapid rise to global prominence so as to explain, if not excuse, the bad geopolitical manners.

In the nineteenth century the doctrine of America's manifest destiny grew to replace and exaggerate the colonial idea that, in Perry Miller's famous phrase, the Massachusetts pilgrims were on God's errand in the wilderness. So long as the Americans kept to themselves, relatively isolated from Europe, American exceptionalism would remain, as Tocqueville seems to have found it, a quaint, if rude, national characteristic. But once the United States was drawn, however reluctantly, into global politics, as it was in the twentieth century, its nationalism went beyond bad manners. America's nationalist messianism had its roots in a foundational principle of the national community. Whether in the religious language of the Massachusetts divines or the quasi-religious doctrine of manifest destiny, American exceptionalism is a truly exceptional illustration of a nation's understanding of its historical purpose as the divine plan for humanity.

The excess of this extreme nationalism was what Niebuhr called, early in the Cold War, the irony of the American situation:

> Our dreams of bringing the whole of human history under the control of the human will are ironically refuted by the fact that no group of idealists can easily move the pattern of history toward the desired goal of peace and justice. The recalcitrant forces in the historical drama have a power and persistence beyond our

reckoning. Our own nation, always a vivid symbol of the most characteristic attitudes of a bourgeois culture, is less potent to do what it wants in the hour of its greatest strength than it was in its infancy.[33]

This was 1952, the year of Niebuhr's stroke, which as he would put it late in life forced him to the sidelines. As he slowly returned to writing and lecturing, it would seem that his attitude toward American nationalism was less forgiving. By 1959, in *The Structure of Nations and Empires*, he was speaking of the United States as an imperial nation alongside Soviet Russia, its hegemonic rival. The post–World War II realities put American nationalism in a global situation for which it was ill-suited—an innocent people now responsible for the world.

Whether it is called imperialism, irony, or messianism, the national ideology was natural to a protestantized culture in which history can be misinterpreted as the purposeful projection of God's will on earth. It denies all possibility of contradiction—not to mention of man's uncertain status as a creature who sins because he cannot stomach the thought of his limits. One of the more bedeviling manifestations of this protestantizing of American political culture is the nation's civil religion.

The idea of civil religion was first used in the modern era by Jean-Jacques Rousseau on the romantic wing of the French Enlightenment. It was then, perhaps still is, a kind of general religious faith in faith that was evident among Deists of the American Enlightenment. Jefferson and Franklin, among others, believed in a god so abstract as to bear little relation to the Christian God in history. Had Jefferson been a doctrinaire

Christian, the language of the Declaration of Independence would have surely fallen on ears deaf to the Anglican Christianity that was one of Britain's most visible presences in the colonies. Much the same is true of Jefferson's neighbor, James Madison, whose Federalist Papers were, and remain, the single most important commentary on the principles of the Constitution of the United States. Still, in the end, said Niebuhr, the Calvinists of Massachusetts joined spiritual forces with the Deists of Virginia to fashion a unique brand of national religion:

> It is particularly remarkable that the two great religious-moral traditions which informed our early life—New England Calvinism and Virginian Deism and Jeffersonianism—arrive at remarkably similar conclusions about the meaning of our national character and destiny. Calvinism may have held too pessimistic views of human nature, and too mechanical views of the providential ordering of human life. But when it assessed the significance of the American experimental both its conceptions of American destiny and its appreciation of American virtue finally arrived at conclusions strikingly similar to those of the Deists. Whether our nation interprets its spiritual heritage through Massachusetts or Virginia, we came into existence with the sense of being a "separated" nation, which God was using to make a new beginning for mankind.[34]

Yet granting the cultural compromises of the Virginia and Massachusetts traditions, a more explicitly Protestant religion would become a distinctive feature of the nation's cultural development after the Revolution. America's civil sphere would long be marked by a sometimes vague, but always necessary, sense of its messianic mission to mankind—a mission bequeathed it by a god of remotely Protestant silhouette.

After the revolutionary era came to a symbolic end with the deaths of Jefferson and Adams on July 4, 1826, religion by whatever name played itself out according to the natural law of religious enthusiasms—fervid at the first, soon enough thereafter tepid; hence the importance of times of renewal and awakening. Even the Great Awakening in Massachusetts and Connecticut in the eighteenth century, while at extreme odds with the rationalism of the early Calvinists and Deists, was in its way characteristic of religion in America.

The First Great Awakening in the 1730s and 1740s broke as a matter of course just before the revolutionary era. Though the fervor had begun among English evangelists like George Whitefield, in America it was Jonathan Edwards (1703–58) of Yale and Northampton who was its voice. Edwards has been called the most important religious thinker in eighteenth-century America.[35] His participation in the Great Awakening of 1730–45 certainly encouraged the movement's cleansing effect on colonial culture in North America and thus bestowed a degree of moral energy to the coming revolution Edwards would not live to see.

Like Niebuhr (who may have been the most important religious figure in twentieth-century America), Edwards focused on the still unresolved dilemma of American settlement culture. Indeed, Edwards thought in a stern theological language, where the dilemma presented itself as the inherent contradiction between the righteous community and the religious piety of the individual. In more overtly political terms the dilemma was at the core of the early movement toward independence—the apparent incommensurability of the demands of the individual for liberty and of the commonwealth for order. Either way the question of power entered into the formula.

In "Sinners in the Hands of an Angry God" (1741), Edwards's most famous sermon, he denounced the powers of this world as unable to assure the obedience of a rebel to the higher powers:

> There is no want of *power* in God to cast wicked men into hell at any moment. Men's hands cannot be strong when God rises up. The strongest have no power to resist him, nor can any deliver out of his hands. He is not only able to cast wicked men into hell, but he can most easily do it. Sometimes an earthly prince meets with a great deal of difficulty to subdue a rebel, who has found means to fortify himself, and has made himself strong by the numbers of his followers. But it is not so with God.[36]

These words are of another time from Niebuhr's, but they are, like Niebuhr's basic theory of the human situation, characteristic of the prophetic messianism associated with religious criticisms of worldly pride. Jonathan Edwards, his times and beliefs aside, was chief among those of his day whose stern pronouncements had the unintended long-term effect of defining a persistent dilemma of subsequent American culture. For Niebuhr the contradiction was between the dangerous power of messianic nationalism and the realism of prophetic messianism.

The dilemma is endemic to democratic societies that claim to focus individual passions against the demanding pull of the commonwealth to conform. In Europe, at about the time of America's First Awakening, the conflict took the form of a struggle between the universalizing principles of Enlightenment and the particularizing feelings of Romanticism. The free individual's feeling of a particular comfort—whether in the intimate address of her god or the familiar tastes of local custom—is almost always procured at a cost to social justice and well-being among members of the societal whole. Though its expressions may be many, the contradictions go with any political territory that pretends to respect the rights and freedoms of the individual. When rights are taken as the protective sheath of the individual's freedom, they inevitably keep the individual from feeling the delicacy of his dependence on the collective for some degree of justice.

This dilemma worked its way out differently in eighteenth-century American colonies, if only because religious fervor was a constant pressing secular reason down from its universalizing claims. Though in America rationalists like Edwards's contemporary Benjamin Franklin won out officially, the piety that particular feeling is the standard of truth never ceded the ground it held in Edwards's time. Today the conflict that haunts public life is the fallen angel of the eighteenth century's spiritual dilemma—the dark ghost that unleashes religious fervor against the constraints of social justice.

Reinhold Niebuhr's stake in this controversy, a good two centuries after Edwards, was that he revived attention to the original contradiction of American culture—between the unyielding demands of social justice and the feelings associated with both religious and political piety. Niebuhr's influence on mid-twentieth-century America was not as dramatic, perhaps, as that of Edwards on the eighteenth, but his times were fraught with upheavals brought on by America's periodic turns to religious revivalism. The 1950s in America may not properly be called a time of domestic religious revival comparable to those of the eighteenth and nineteenth centuries. But the Cold War did ignite a very American nationalist fervor in which the struggle with communism assumed all of the markings of a messianism in which America was meant to save humanity from a nuclear and ideological Armageddon. The crude thinking at all levels of American politics from Kennan to the followers of McCarthy was a contraction of the nation's soul—one that was presented in secular terms that eventually masked the religious enthusiasms that swept over the political landscape—first in the insanity of the anticommunist fervors, then slowly in the resurgence of the Nixon era, which rapidly led to the full-blown political mania of the religious right in the last two decades of the twentieth century.

By the 1950s Niebuhr's political philosophy had grown both more mature and more sharply realist, and nowhere more so than with respect to the irony of America's global situation in the Cold War:

> Tragic elements in the present situation are not as significant as the ironic ones. Pure tragedy elicits tears of admiration and pity for the hero who is willing to brave death or incur guilt for the sake of some great good. Irony however prompts some laughter and a nod of comprehension beyond the laughter; for irony involves comic absurdities which cease to be absurd when fully understood. Our age is involved in irony because so many dreams of our nation have been so cruelly refuted by history. Our dreams of a pure virtue are dissolved in a situation in which it is possible to exercise the virtue

of responsibility toward a community of nations only by courting the prospective guilt of the atomic bomb. And the irony is increased by the frantic efforts of some idealists to escape this hard reality by dreaming up schemes of an ideal world order which have no relevance to either our present dangers or our urgent duties.[37]

Reading these words more than a half-century later, the situational details being changed, one marvels at their pertinence to the American situation in the twenty-first century—greater power in relation to the rest of world than it had after World War II, and correspondingly less ability to manage the global reach of its claim to moral authority.

In "Civil Religion in America" (1967), Robert Bellah cast a strikingly Christian interpretation on the turning points of American political life—none more obvious than his theory of the Civil War and of Abraham Lincoln as, in a word, America's Christ of the Union's death and resurrection:

With the Civil War, a new theme of death, sacrifice, and rebirth enters the new civil religion. It is symbolized in the life and death of Lincoln. Nowhere is it stated more vividly than in the Gettysburg Address, itself part of the Lincolnian "New Testament" among the civil scriptures. Robert Lowell has recently pointed out the "insistent use of birth images" in this speech explicitly devoted to "these honored dead": "brought forth," "conceived," "created," "a new birth of freedom."[38]

In the 1960s Bellah's civil-religion essay sparked a considerable interest, especially among younger students of religion who were, at the time, baffled by the secular awakening of the time, when new forms of consciousness drew the young into an unruly mix of political activism and countercultural nonsense. The seriousness of Bellah's idea would be borne out by a conservative evangelical movement in the 1980s and 1990s that rose to the center of national power in the 2000s.

Walter Russell Mead, in "God's Country?" (2006), has argued that the evangelical movements of the 2000s might be considered a Great Awakening of their own kind. He makes the telling claim that the differences among evangelicals, fundamentalists, and mainstream liberal faiths are real, but, whatever the differences, these faiths also share many of the religious principles associated with the Protestant principle. He adds that the apparently wild divergences among them are part of a constantly sifting Protestant culture in America that remains powerfully influential in the country's political life because "Protestantism has shaped much of the country's identity and remains today the majority faith in the United States."[39]

On balance, the history of American civil religion is one that Niebuhr, without using the phrase, understood well in 1932:

The evolutionary optimism of the eighteenth and nineteenth century, and the sentimentalism of the moral and social problem in romanticism, have affected religious idealism with particular force in America, because they suited the mood of a youthful and vigorous people, youth usually being oblivious to the brutality which is the inevitable concomitant of vitality. Furthermore, the expanding economy of America obscured the cruelties of the class struggle in our economic life, and the comparative isolation of a continent made the brutalities of international conflict less obvious. In spite of the disillusionment of the World War, the average liberal Protestant Christian is still convinced that the kingdom of God is gradually approaching.[40]

Niebuhr's method allowed him to interpret social phenomena as constantly shifting, ever vulnerable to transposition, never purely perfect. Liberal religion, in 1932, meant one thing. But American religious roots in a ubiquitous Protestant culture meant that, then as now, the liberal idea of progress comes back to haunt the American body politic.

When faced with a ghost one must choose either to run from it or to confront it. The ironic history of America is that it has been so disposed to run from the truth of history's contradictions. The Cold War may have at the time seemed to be an exceptional crisis in a nation that had come to think in terms of exceptions. More to the facts of the matter, the Cold War and all that it engendered, including the catastrophic foreign policy that led to 9/11, then, in aftereffect, to wars the Americans *had* to win at a time against a situation when and where winning is more difficult to define than ever before.

In such a time, the question before the Americans is one Niebuhr put to earlier expressions of the American irony. Were the Depression, the war of 1941, the Cold War crises independent of each other, thus apart from the crisis of the 2000s? Niebuhr would have surely said they were not. His was a deeply structural method—one that probed not just to the deepest possible sources of historical change but to the deepest *and* most realistic ones. Time and time again America's religious culture— whether civil or sectarian—has contributed importantly to its special nature among the nations of human history. At the same time it has worked against the nation's ability to face the ghost of its unusual creativity.

What is to be done, now? Niebuhr, of course, could not have provided a road map out of the structural crisis, the early forms of which he diagnosed. But he did provide an ethical and political orientation to human history that might, at this late date, save the day.

6

political recovery and globalization

knowing the difference

Words Reinhold Niebuhr first uttered sometime in the 1930s or 1940s are recurrently thought to have been the words of anyone but him—St. Francis of Assisi, a German who claimed the right to them, some unknown author.[1] The words are familiar the world over as the Serenity Prayer:

> God grant me the serenity
> to accept the things I cannot change;
> courage to change the things I can;
> and wisdom to know the difference.

The prayer has been adopted by Alcoholics Anonymous and other twelve-step programs for recovery from addictions of all kinds. Every day and night of the year, nearly anyplace on earth, there are meetings of anonymous individuals attempting to overcome life-destroying addictions. The words, recited in unison usually at the beginning of meetings, summarize the key first steps toward a life in recovery:

1. We admitted we were powerless over alcohol—that our lives had become unmanageable.
2. Came to believe that a Power greater than ourselves could restore us to sanity.
3. Made a decision to turn our will and our lives over to the care of God *as we understood Him.*

A recovery program (as it is called), turns on the ability of the individual to admit to powerlessness over the addicting substance, then to turn his life over to a god—or, a higher power, which is to say: a god the person willing to change his life can believe in. The first step is the hardest because it is not even a little bit easy to admit to ourselves that we can no longer control our lives. None of the steps is easy. Most who try fail at first. Many try again and again. Some succeed in doing nothing more than— and this is important—understanding themselves as powerless, unable to control themselves, willing to continue day by day in a permanent life of recovery.

Recovery programs, beginning with Alcoholics Anonymous, adopted Niebuhr's Serenity Prayer as a mantra because it so well expresses a proven formula for success in a lifelong struggle with the grip of addiction. June 10, 1935, is considered the date of the founding of AA. Thus the program's principles did not come directly from Niebuhr.[2] The principles of Alcoholics Anonymous were taken from an informal Christian group—the Oxford Group in the United Kingdom.[3] As for the Serenity Prayer, there is no getting around the religious theme of its message. Yet what it conveys is a universal truth of the human situation—one that reaches well beyond its Christian elements. William James, for one who was not emphatically Christian, had the experience of discovering the human value of powerlessness and thus the need of a higher power.[4] Higher powers, like gods, can come in many forms, none entirely easy to fathom.[5]

Reinhold Niebuhr's daughter, Elisabeth Sifton, has explained that Alcoholics Anonymous softened the harder terms of the prayer her father wrote in 1943.[6] The prayer, as he wrote it, apparently for the first time, for a rural church near his vacation home in Heath, Massachusetts, is this:

> God, give us grace to accept with serenity
> the things that *cannot* be changed,
> Courage to change the things
> which *should* be changed,
> and the Wisdom to distinguish
> the one from the other.

Sifton explains that there are two crucial differences between her father's version and the one adopted by Alcoholics Anonymous. Niebuhr's version—"God give us grace to accept with serenity the things that *cannot* be changed"—is simpler but also more direct to the point of his religious thinking. Where the popular version petitions for serenity to accept the things "we cannot change," Niebuhr insisted on the theological point that there are things that "cannot *be* changed," least of all by those who are powerless. More seriously, Niebuhr's second line is a petition for "courage to change the things which *should* be changed" and, again, not just (as in the popular version) "to change what we can." Sifton puts it right:

> But there are circumstances that *should be changed* yet may seem beyond our powers to alter, and these are the changes under which the prayer is most needed. The shift in the text [in the popular version] reduces a difficult, strong idea to a banal, weak one, and I suspect that this dumbing down of the prayer has contributed to its enormous popularity.[7]

This was one of Niebuhr's essential insights into human nature—that we will always dumb down the difficult.

Though the Serenity Prayer was written (as distinct from spoken) relatively late in Reinhold Niebuhr's active career—some fifteen years into his time at Union Seminary in New York—it stands, in its original form, as a better-than-good-enough representation of the man's thinking.

One of Niebuhr's more touching self-insights comes from a personal statement, written in 1967 but never published in his lifetime. He had but four years to live. Here Niebuhr sums up the basic achievements of his life as a preacher, political activist, author of the Serenity Prayer and of many important books, and much else. The 1967 memoir is affecting because Niebuhr, near the end of his days, retained his capacity for honest self-criticism. He wrote of his embarrassment that, after the stroke and his infirmity, he was unable to live up to his moral teachings. He wrote candidly of his anxiety and depression at the loss of physical strength, and of his fear of death—thus too of his struggle to accept with serenity the things that could not be changed. Still, Niebuhr could affirm the ironies of the evangelical Gospel that "faith in an incomprehensible divine source of order was an indispensable bearer of the human trust in life, despite the evils of nature and the incongruities of history."[8] Such is the irony that sustains a life like Niebuhr's: recognizing the possibilities in the limits; speaking honestly of the good without being able, or willing, to sort the wheat from the weeds.

Deeper still, the Serenity Prayer and its suitability to the ideals of a program meant to help people accept the limits of their power in order to change what should be changed captures the main idea of his greatest book, *Nature and Destiny of Man:* "This wisdom about our destiny is dependent upon a humble recognition of the limits of our knowledge and our power."[9]

Karl Marx recklessly referred to religion as an opiate of the people. What he did not quite capture in that one line was that, if this were true of religion, then also of political ideas, including his own. Marx knew next to nothing about religion, which for him was an empty category. He meant to rid the modern world of all otherworldly ideologies that might cause the working poor to overlook their plight in this world. Worse yet, he thought he knew quite a lot about politics. Again he was reckless. One might overlook the silliness of Marx's dismissal of religions, one and all, had he rested his case with the brilliant critique of modern capitalism. Instead, by dithering in political theory, he left himself open to the very criticism he would have least expected.

Niebuhr nailed Marx on the contradictions of his political theory by condemning it as just another modernizing ideology that denied the realities of history—not perhaps as terrible as being called bourgeois, but for Marx the next worst thing. Niebuhr was not the kind of person who would dwell on Marx's drug metaphor, but he might well have approved of its application to the state of modern political thought.

One of the lessons Niebuhr offers the early twenty-first century is the recognition that the twentieth century as it came to be an American century slid sickeningly into a political mess of its own doing. What he teaches still is that the history he observed so probingly in his times may be past in calendrical time, but its consequences persist in historical time. The irony of American history from the Depression in the 1930s, through wars hot and cold in the 1940s and 1950s, to the new social movements and Vietnam in the 1960s, down to the present time lies in the nation's chronic inability to adjust its thinking to the realities of its global power. America was then an innocent nation in an innocent world. The world today may not be notably adult, but it is no longer innocent—least of all in regard to the limits of any nation's power. Europe is ready at least to put nationalism behind it. East Asia's nations are flexible as to the exceptions their states grant for the sake of economic gain.[10] Even Russia is a dangerous work in progress that now depends on its oil and trade lines to the West. Only the United States totters uneasily in an ideological stupor. Innocence and power, as Niebuhr said in the 1950s, is a dangerous combination when the two come together in a nation that thinks itself superior to all others.

To be intoxicated with self is to exaggerate power. Sooner or later a punk sneaks up and hits you in the balls. More elegantly, Niebuhr might have said that the crisis of the Cold War era came about because America at the time was but a proud farm boy of a nation, naïve as to the limits of its muscle, morally unsure as to its adult responsibilities. If that then, is it not just so today? America's catastrophic failures to recognize how it has wasted its power and wealth haunt its friends and inspire its enemies. September 11, 2001, was a blow to the nation's nether parts.

Nations, as Niebuhr taught, are not often able to see beyond their interests. They can on occasion, if only for a while, and then only when coerced by crisis. Europe and East Asia since 1945 have to a detectable degree. But America among the powers of the world has stubbornly refused—or perhaps been unable—to look deeply at its behavior. Yet season after season, political leaders in America romanticize the past of a greatest generation when Americans fought and won their wars. At the highest levels of government, the nation is paralyzed by what from time to time is still called the Vietnam Syndrome—a "reluctance to win at war." The illusion of a victory not gained in Vietnam haunts its policies in Iraq. Leaders of both parties, small differences being granted, are locked in the straitjacket of American innocence. There are exceptions, of course, and some hope for a different future. But whatever happens as a new century presses on, if the nation is to get over its ideological frustrations with the real limits of its power, it will be not by renewal but by recovery—a break from the past that redeems the national philosophy.

Until (and unless) that happens, the United States, hence the world it continues to influence, will suffer the effects of an ideological opiate—the belief that good individuals make for a good nation so long as their markets are free, their work is hard, and their resources limitless.

Was the Cold War, from 1946 to 1991, a forty-five-year interruption in the natural ebb and flow of human history? Or was it the normal course of history, as Niebuhr understood it—always hurtling toward ends that cannot be foreseen, constantly torn by the possibilities for human creativity and the realities of human pride?

A half-century and more on, some believe that, troubles aside, the world, if not all its nations, is on the road to recovery from the most terrible of centuries, the twentieth. Their confidence is based on the promises of globalization understood as a closing of global ranks around the demands of economic markets. China and India depend on access to the North American consumer and service markets. China alone could bring down the U.S. economy were it to sell its dollar reserves for euros. No one believes it will because China's economy depends on its economic relations with the rest of the world, which in turn requires the Americans to do well. Europe can experiment with a postnationalist community that is not a supranational power because the United States pays for Europe's defense, which it does because, after World War II, America unthinkingly agreed to be the world's policeman. Now it spends 40 percent of its tax dollars on its military—more in real dollars than the next eight military powers combined. The United States in some ways cannot keep itself from military misadventures like Vietnam and Iraq if only because its national interests are so vested in its military presence around the world. Whatever may have been its interests in oil in the Middle East, America had first to protect its bases and ports that are the lifelines of its global presence.

In retrospect would the United States have been better off at the end of World War II had it resisted the responsibility of being then the only global industrial power and one of two military giants? Who can say? When America does good, as it undoubtedly did in World War II, then it is responsible for what it has done. It this respect, whatever good a nation may do is never simply a question of altruism but, as Niebuhr thought, that nation's interest in the business of doing business. The United States rebuilt Germany and Japan after the war at least as much because it needed them as buyers for its industrial products. Nations, if they do good, do good as icing on the cake. But the cake is main thing. In the 1940s the cake was economic. Could the United States, had it had a less innocent temperament, have paused before engaging the Soviets, then the Chinese, in the Cold War? Economically—which is to say: militarily— probably not. There would have been no point to rebuilding Japan and Germany only then to give away the Korean Peninsula and Berlin, much less the Middle East and Africa.

The historical question of the Cold War is not, however, whether the United States could have stayed out of it in the long run. Given what America was then, and had been for a long time already, the answer almost certainly is no. The better question is whether America might not have engaged less innocently. This is a hard question to answer because doing so would have required, under a tremendous global pressure of responsibility, a near immediate maturation of its global philosophy. Individuals are known to be capable of this. Niebuhr did it upon the death of his father. But nations are less able to probe what inner souls they may have. In this respect, America's prolonged philosophical immaturity was forced upon it by the uneven history of the world in the twentieth century.

Niebuhr's view was that it was not just America but the whole of the West that was innocent. The United States was the one stuck with the necessity and the responsibility. Europe, it now seems, learned from the tragedy of the forty-year war from 1914 to 1945. It is one thing to project power, another to have it projected on you. Europe's experience underground gave it time for reassessment—a time prolonged by the extended period of reconstruction after the war. The Americans, however, did not have history on their side. Not only were they reluctant to enter the first war, of 1914, but after they disarmed to dance through the 1920s. The crash of 1929 caught them ill-prepared, again. They had become the power of the global economy but with no sense of how benignly to engage the world it now needed for its own sense of economic well-being. When the United States was crippled economically through the 1930s, had it not been for Franklin Roosevelt it might not have pulled itself together in time to meet the challenge of the second war, of the 1940s. That done in 1945, only months later Stalin surprised the Americans still again by being what he had always been—a petulant, hard-nosed tyrant.

Had America had (or taken) time, it might have called Stalin's bluff without exciting too much its trigger-happy self-regard. The most you can hope for from an innocent in such a circumstance is that he get through the worst of it, then move along to the sophomore year. But in the Cold War the United States was not even sophomoric. It was too confident as to what it was and was meant to be. Victory at war and industrial development in the early 1940s certified America's faith in its foundational idea of its providential duties. To be sophomoric is to talk too much without knowing how stupid you sound. Still, that is better than a silent, wrong-headed determination. Perhaps had the Americans spent the late 1940s and 1950s talking among themselves, even to others, including the Soviets, they might have bought some time to do what the Europeans had been forced to do more or less since 1914.

When Niebuhr identified the fate of man as a consequence of human pride and selfishness, he was describing a sober but not deterministic theory of human history. History is in human hands until it is not. The question to ask is how do we respond when it is not? Messianism, one might say, is the trickster of human history—the shape-shifting element that plays at the limits, setting ends against the middle. Messiahs may be actual prophetic figures in a religious tradition, but they may also be harbingers of a more generic kind. Any surprising event or pattern of events that gathers force in the public imagination can call to mind the prospect that human communities, like the individuals that constitute them, are finite. The expectation that history will come, in time, to an ending can lead in any number of directions. But in the twentieth century one messianic idea dominated.

For Niebuhr the century of full-blown industrial capitalism was driven by what he called messianic nationalism—the age-old allure of empires and nations to think of themselves as the fulfillment of history, thus of themselves as the end of humankind and the perfection of man's nature. Against overblown nationalisms, Niebuhr set prophetic messianism—a category that to some today may remain troubling. Niebuhr unflinchingly understood prophetic messianism as a biblical view of human history. But Niebuhr also, like Augustine, from whom he took his inspiration, allowed that messianism can reach beyond any particular religious line.

When Giorgio Agamben, referring to the current situation, said that the modern world needs a messiah, he was drawing on the classical tradition of prophetic messianism that can be traced back from Niebuhr, through Luther, Augustine, and Paul, to the prophets of Ancient Israel.[11] For Agamben, writing in Italy in 2000, on the eve of 9/11, the messiah needed was the trickster that, whatever its epiphany, might stun the modernist world into recognition that its self-satisfied respect for its own political ideals is, contrary to its belief, built on the principle that the state is a state because it can suspend its own laws. "The fundamental activity," said Agamben, "of the sovereign power is the production of bare life as the originary political element."[12] No exceptions. States manage the border between inclusion and exclusion, which, in this world, is the border between the bene-fits of citizenship and the social death of the camps and slums. This is a severe idea that would be intolerable were it not that the history of the twentieth century was a history most violent—war upon war, exclusion upon exclusion, resulting in more than half of the world's six billion–plus people living outside the liberal limits of human decency.

This is the other side of globalization—and the side that Niebuhr would have taken, though not without agony at the misery it has created. Optimists think the globalizing world is good because it is so fast and so resplendent with possibilities for real human contact across differences. They are not wrong. In fact, they are right to the extent that, were it possible to imagine FDR and Stalin not in Yalta but emailing one another, even the very ill FDR might have been able to see through the sham that led to the partitioning of Europe. By 1962, JFK was agile enough to deploy a kind of proto-email communication when he ignored Khrushchev's first menacing letter in the Cuban missile crisis and chose to respond only to the second more temperate one as if the first had not existed. "Sorry," we say today, "but it must have gone to my spam folder." The slippage, even in a world of speed, can buy the time to pause and come to one's better senses. Globalization is far from a bad thing.

But globalization, being speed above all else, can also leave the masses behind, as it has, while also creating the illusion that the new and wondrous fast life in, say, Beijing is the all, which entails a functional ignorance of the bare life in the Pearl River hinter-lands. We cannot know what Niebuhr would have thought of this aspect of the current situation. He was, in his time, one of a very few true globalists not in the employ of the Kremlin or the State Department. He assuredly interpreted the Cold War in global terms—stipulating the Americans and the Soviets as hegemonic powers controlling a split and torn global order.

But even more to the point of the present situation, I think Niebuhr would have understood the possibilities that globalization imposes on national politics. By possibilities he, most decidedly, would not have meant promises to make the material world better. His faith would have kept his eye on the promises that issue from a time of stocktaking forced upon individuals, groups, or nations by events beyond their power to control. This may have been the benefit Europe gained from the forty-year war with Germany. Riskier to say so, but it might also have been an unanticipated consequence of the economic and social failures of the Maoist period culminating in the nightmare of the Cultural Revolution from 1966 to 1976. Either way, nothing in America's Cold War, or in the political and cultural disruptions of the 1960s, had this effect. Beginning in 1968 through at least 2008, national politics in America were dominated by a Right of classically liberal ideas that meant to reestablish the old-time individualist values of the Republic.

Not even the Clinton interregnum of 1992–2000 could be counted as a time of relief and reflection on the deeper meanings of America. Clinton's third-way neoliberalism served the mammon of prosperity administered by policy genius that led him and his party no farther than the nose of the next election cycle. Clinton and Reagan were two faces of the same free-market individualistic moral coin. One thought he brought down that wall. The other believed he broke the barrier that kept the poor from progress. Neither gave more than a passing thought to the prospect that America's liberal culture might have come to the asymptote of its maximum progressive utility. The one played the bluff of a trickle-down condescension that enriched the already wealthy. The other puffed up the ingratiating nonsense that what happens in Davos will not stay in Davos, where he and Bono passed out the bromides of their very good intentions. Meanwhile neoliberal trade accords amounted, in real economic terms, to the same effect as trickle-down. The excluded, since the 1980s, grew in numbers the most free of economic imaginations cannot admit—that, among other astonishing facts, a small number of super-rich individuals have more wealth than most of the world's population; or that a billion people worldwide live as squatters in camps or *biddonvilles*.

Somewhere along the vector of a history where humanity divides into a small number of those included and a much larger mass of those on the margins of life itself, it may be fair to expect a rude awakening. If not that, then perhaps the creep of global warming, the closeness of starvation to the bourgeois doorsteps, the threat of blood transfers through the HIV pool, the continuing civil violence, more still, might be what Niebuhr would have seen as a possibility.

What kind of possibility? That, simply, of coming to the recognition that, as human animals, we live to do what we do and will die—that, at the least, the resources we require for the most elemental needs of survival are finite and that, in a word, history does not move inexorably toward some perfect state of good or better. The possibility that Niebuhr might have depicted is that of realizing that how we think and act determines our fate. Our fate is not in our hands but, as creative creatures, we can measure it and come to terms with it. This we cannot do by clinging to the old lifelines—and especially not the lifeline of liberal/conservative/neoliberal culture that, by whichever name, has so stupefied the collective mind that the masses are unable to walk a straight line. When collective life becomes a sobriety test, then it is time for a new program—one that Niebuhr's best-known words may help to do its work.

Is it too, too strange to speak of political recovery? Of, that is, admitting that what we moderns—and especially we modern or postmodern Americans—have thought of as the principles of our special nature are, it turns out, spent? Is it possible for a liberal culture—meaning, again, the whole of the main political movements of the European Diaspora since the eighteenth century—to bring itself to its senses, if not quite its knees?

If there is an obvious gain to be taken from globalization, whichever view of it one holds, it is that the global realities put the modern order of political and social truths in some considerable doubt—a doubt that rides on the winds of a near-perfect storm. For one thing, the nation-state can no longer be thought of as the defining unit of the political. Some say the nation-state must fade before the global order. This remains to be seen. What is clear is that no nation can afford to do as America tried to do until 1941, then failed to comprehend after 1945. Globally, not even the most powerful can go it alone or anything like alone. The Chinese, today, seem to understand this reality principle better than the Americans.

For another, insofar as globalization has come to pass on an economic ideology of permanent growth, it forces those who will face realities to admit, as many are doing, that the planet's resources are not limitless. There is no new technological or investment strategy that will continue, as the liberals say, creating jobs forever out of the whole cloth of pollution and warming.

For a third, participation in the global order, for those who can or must, requires people to accept the limiting realities of social differences. Whether they move to Shanghai or Dublin because they are cool cities or are forced to flee to the mountains of Pakistan or the arid plains of Chad because they must, wherever they go people of all economic stations run up against the limits of their familiar languages, traditions, and cultures. And on goes the list.

Will the globally obvious necessarily cause the human community to reorder its thoughts, to redirect its actions, to reconsider its naïve assumptions? Niebuhr would have said it can happen if, and only if, we (and this is hard) accept our sinful nature— accept, that is, the proven reality that human nature is proud and self-satisfied. Modern liberal cultures have merely perfected the art of self-preoccupation and greed by convincing the many that a utopia is there to be had in the hard work of striving for the pure social order in which we all are meant to own whatever we need or desire. Utopias are truly no place to be found.

Serenity can come from knowing the difference between who one is (or what a people are) and what they think they might be (or wish they were). The trick to a life of wisdom, whether individual or collective, is to accept the difference, thus to relax into the daily grind of changing what must be changed. The hardest thing in this life is to believe, truly believe, that one is powerless to control life itself. Individuals, Niebuhr taught, are of a different order from societies. But this applies most acutely, he said, to the equation whereby the moral sensibilities of individuals are assumed to be the same as those of large social wholes.

Today the equation may be reversible. Globalization, among its many still uncertain meanings, amounts to the reality that no one economic or political power can control its own destiny. The limits that globalization literally brings home to nations, resources, and cultures might just be the shock that could teach the recovery lesson—that the old must pass away for a new to be born. Individuals do take this in better than large social wholes because in the search for life itself they can come to understand much better than the powers that be just how terrible it is not to be able to control one's own destiny.

Politics may or may not be the art of the possible. But if it is, then, in a time of bare life, when global realities truly put us all in the same boat, then what individuals can on occasion learn might mature into a global recognition of the truth Niebuhr believed was the basic truth of history. Human history is the irony that we know things we cannot do; we do things we are unwilling to think. Life is not tragedy but irony, which can be shocking even when it makes us laugh with a weirdly human sort of joy.

> Joy is closer to God than seriousness. Why?
> Because when I am serious I tend to be self-centered,
> But when I am joyful I tend to forget myself.

—Krister Stendhal (1914–2008)

notes

1. David Brooks, "Obama, Gospel, and Verse," *New York Times*, April 26, 2007. This column was picked up by a number of sources. A Pew Research Center Publication reminded readers that President Jimmy Carter is also an avid reader of Niebuhr; see "Obama's Favorite Theologian? A Short Course on Reinhold Niebuhr," June 26, 2009; http://pewresearch.org/pubs/1268/reinhold-neihbuhr-obama-favorite-theologian. Even before Brooks, Public Radio featured a long interview with the political and religious philosopher Jean Bethke Elshtain on the importance of Niebuhr; December 8, 2004; http://being.publicradio.org/programs/niebuhr-rediscovered/interview-elshtain.shtml.

2. For one among many comments on the Niebuhrian theme in Obama's Nobel Prize speech on December 10, 2009, see George Packer, "Peace and War," *New Yorker*, December 21–28, 2009, 45.

3. For a short history and commentary on the revival, see Paul Elie, "A Man for All Reasons," *Atlantic*, November 2007, 83–96.

4. The most famous of his writings is the short Serenity Prayer, widely used in churches and twelve-step programs and in respect to which there has long been a controversy as to its origins. Curiously, a Yale University librarian, with time on his hands, traced the databases

now available for evidence that it may not have been Niebuhr's prayer. Remarkably, the librarian (also editor of *The Yale Book of Quotations*), never bothered to consider the evidence that the prayer (as we shall see) almost perfectly expressed Niebuhr's uniquely definitive religious theories. See Laurie Goodstein, "Serenity Prayer Stirs up Doubt on Who Wrote It," *New York Times*, July 11, 2008. After a Duke University librarian uncovered evidence that the prayer was Niebuhr's, his Yale counterpart recanted.

5. For a first-rate summary of the place of evangelical movements in American political and foreign policy, see Walter Russell Mead, "God's Country," *Foreign Affairs* 85, no. 5 (September–October 2006), 24–44. Mead is also one of the most notable foreign policy experts to have seriously read Reinhold Niebuhr; see Mead, *God and Gold* (New York: Random House, 2007), 387–402.

6. For an excellent brief summary of "declinism" (coupled with a coherent conservative defense of American global power), see Josef Joffe, "The Default Power: The False Prophecy of America's Decline," *Foreign Affairs* 88, no. 5 (September–October 2009), 21–35. On the other hand, hardly a day goes by without one or another cogent statement of the arguments for a decline of the West and the rise of the East, for example: Niall Ferguson, "The Decade the World Tilted East," *Financial Times*, December 28, 2009, 9.

7. Still the best short summary of the troubling differences among theories of globalization is Stanley Hoffman, "Class of Globalizations," *Foreign Affairs* 81, no. 4 (August–September 2002), 104–15.

CHAPTER ONE:
REINHOLD NIEBUHR

1. Richard Wightman Fox, *Reinhold Niebuhr: A Biography* (New York: Pantheon, 1985), 4.

2. One systematic study of 487 pastors' children over the age of twenty-five found that the single strongest influence on their adult religious lives of the experience in the pastoral home was their "perception

that more was expected of him or her." See Carole Brousson Anderson, "The Experience of Growing Up in a Parsonage," *Pastoral Psychology* 46 (July 1998), 393.

3. This quotation and the references and quotation following are from June Bingham, *Courage to Change: An Introduction to the Life and Thought of Reinhold Niebuhr* (New York: Scribner, 1961), 58–60. For a tendentious view of the father's authoritarian streak, see Fox, *Reinhold Niebuhr*, 3–6.

4. Quoted in Bingham, *Courage*, 58, from the Columbia University Oral History Project.

5. Their numbers are densest in the near Middle West of the United States from Pennsylvania in the East to Missouri in the West, including therefore Ohio, Indiana, and Illinois and, to the north, Iowa, Michigan, Wisconsin, and Minnesota. In 2000 roughly 15 percent of Americans were of German descent. Of this total, forty-three million, about 40 percent are today in these states. In 1892, when Niebuhr was born in Wright City, the concentration was much higher. This was before Germans, like many other European immigrants to the Plains, moved on from the depleted Middle West to the far South, Florida, and the far West, California and Washington (1890 data).

6. Reinhold Niebuhr, *The Messenger* (1957), Reinhold Niebuhr Papers, Library of Congress, Washington, D.C., Box 17 (folder unmarked).

7. "Delta Cooperative Farm," Reinhold Niebuhr Papers, Box 4.

8. Reinhold Niebuhr, "A View of Life from the Sidelines" in *The Essential Reinhold Niebuhr*, ed. Robert McAfee Brown (New Haven: Yale University Press, 1986). The reflection was written in 1967, four years before his death, and not published until 1984.

9. Reinhold Niebuhr, *Man's Nature and His Communities* (New York: Scribner, 1965), includes, at the start, one of his several fragmentary intellectual memoirs in which, as the years went on, he expressed quite a number of self-critical corrections, such as the "unpardonable pedagogical error" of defining man's self-regard as "original sin" in *Nature and Destiny of Man* (New York: Scribner, 1941–43). It is indeed

an unusual person who, infirm and nearing the end, is able not just to correct himself but to do so in an essay that takes account of the current literature on human psychology ("Self-Seeking and Self-Giving," in *Man's Nature*).

10. *Leaves* is an edited version of the journal Niebuhr kept during the Detroit years; Reinhold Niebuhr, *Leaves from the Notebook of a Tamed Cynic* (Chicago: Willett, Clark, and Colby, 1929), 3. Years listed parenthetically in passages from *Leaves* correspond to Niebuhr's notations of the year of the journal entry.

11. Ibid., 1.

12. Ibid., 17.

13. Ibid., 43.

14. Walter Rauschenbusch, *A Theology for the Social Gospel* (New York: Macmillan, 1917), 5.

15. Ibid., 228.

16. Washington Gladden, "O Master, Let Me Walk with Thee" (1879). Gladden was of course more of the Midwest and of an earlier generation, which would explain the more forthright piety of his thinking that would be evident in his prose writing at a much later date than the famous hymn: "We believe that the race question and the labor question and the trust question and the liquor question and the graft question and all the other questions will find a speedy solution when men have learned to walk in the way of Jesus." See Gladden, *The Church and Modern Life* (Boston: Houghton, Mifflin and Company, 1908), chapter 8. Still, writing in 1917 (the year before Gladden died), with war and injustice before him, Rauschenbusch held to the goodness of man and the forward progress of the race—though clearly in a less overtly pious (and more Baptist) formulation than Gladden's.

17. On Niebuhr's transformation from Social Gospel liberalism to political realism, still the best book is Donald Meyer, *The Protestant Search for Political Realism, 1919–1941*, 2nd ed. (Middletown, Conn.: Wesleyan University Press, 1988). See also John C. Bennett, "Reinhold Niebuhr's Social Ethics," in *Reinhold Niebuhr: His Religious, Social, and Political Thought*, ed. Charles W. Kegley and Robert W. Bretall

(New York: Macmillan, 1956), 45–78, and Niebuhr's reply at the end of the book.

18. Niebuhr, *Leaves*, 197–98.

19. Ibid., Preface, x.

20. John C. Dancy to Reinhold Niebuhr, April 30, 1928 in Reinhold Niebuhr Papers, Box 55, folder marked "Bethel Evangelical."

CHAPTER TWO:
EVANGELICAL PREACHER

1. For an intellectually sympathetic discussion of Niebuhr's critique of liberal thought in America see Arthur Schlesinger, Jr., "Reinhold Niebuhr's Role in American Political Thought," in *Reinhold Niebuhr: His Religious, Social, and Political Thought*, ed. Charles W. Kegley and Robert W. Bretall (New York: Macmillan, 1956), 125–50.

2. Arthur Schlesinger, Jr., "Forgetting Reinhold Niebuhr," *New York Times Book Review*, September 18, 2005, 12.

3. Reinhold Niebuhr, *The Irony of American History* (New York: Scribner, 1952).

4. June Bingham, *Courage to Change: An Introduction to the Life and Thought of Reinhold Niebuhr* (New York: Scribner, 1961), 3

5. I owe this to Donald Meyer, a self-professed affiliate of Atheists for Niebuhr, at a seminar in the Department of Religion at Wesleyan University, April 2005.

6. Francis Fitzgerald, "The New Evangelicals: A Growing Challenge to the Religious Right," *New Yorker*, June 30, 2008.

7. Among other places, see Harold Bloom, *Jesus and Yahweh, The Names Divine* (New York: Riverhead, 2005).

8. Reinhold Niebuhr, "The Assurance of Grace," in *The Essential Reinhold Niebuhr*, ed. Robert McAfee Brown (New Haven: Yale University Press, 1986), 62.

9. Then, more, the New Testament includes (for reasons not entirely obvious) other letters. There are several attributed to James (possibly the brother of Jesus), to John, to Peter (who may have been the Peter of

the original twelve disciples); and Hebrews (often but improbably attributed to Paul); and some lesser letters also assigned on far from impressive grounds to Paul: Timothy, Titus, and Philemon; plus a tiny epistle from Jude. Then, too, there is the inscrutable Revelation to John, a collection of apocalyptic visions, which is read seriously only by those who appreciate weird riddles and overcoded predictions.

10. This is what Paul Tillich, Niebuhr's friend and fellow theologian, called the Protestant Principle, in *The Protestant Era* (Chicago: University of Chicago Press, 1948), chapter 11.

11. Quoted in Elisabeth Sifton, *The Serenity Prayer* (New York: Norton, 2003), 308.

12. This is view of his daughter, Elisabeth Sifton, ibid., 145–46.

13. In an admittedly informal survey of the sermon outlines and notes during the Detroit years, the Wheat and the Tares appeared twice. When the general theme is taken into account, it appears many more times. Only the question for the future of modern civilization appears more often; see Reinhold Niebuhr Papers, Box 14, files 8, 9, 10, 13. Among the edited collections of Niebuhr's writings, including sermons, this sermon is included prominently in Ursula Niebuhr, *Justice and Mercy* (New York: Harper and Row, 1974), and Brown, *The Essential Reinhold Niebuhr*. In both cases the editors, his widow and one of his most famous students, include a version of the sermon as it was preached at Union Theological Seminary in 1960. The sermon was also preached, in a different form, at the Heath Church sometime in the 1940s. The 1960 version is also included in the Reinhold Niebuhr Audio Collection, CD N665 11–13 (Union Theological Seminary and Presbyterian School of Christian Education, Richmond, Va.). In other words, the Wheat and the Tares text was used often beginning no later than 1922 (the earliest version dated in the Library of Congress texts). The significance, however, is not in these facts so much as in the centrality of the parable's theme to his basic theological position, even before it had been fully developed. All biblical quotations are from the King James Version.

14. The joke occurs in the recording of his sermons and is confirmed by Elisabeth Sifton.

15. Psalms 90:6 was another text Niebuhr read more than once.

16. Reinhold Niebuhr, "The Wheat and the Tares," in Ursula Niebuhr, *Justice and Mercy*, 59.

17. There is something weirdly out of touch about books that proclaim God a delusion or propose to reveal how religion poisons everything—written, respectively, by a scientist who assumes that theology is child's play and a literate professional crank who believes that anything having to do with belief is mindless. Arguments of this kind appear in each age—always with reference to the evil done in the name of religion, cast in the form of final truth; hence: Richard Dawkins, *The God Delusion* (Boston: Houghton Mifflin, 2006), and Christopher Hitchens, *God Is Not Great: How Religion Poisons Everything* (New York: Twelve/Hatchette, 2007).

CHAPTER THREE:
POWERS, PULPITS, AND
POLITICS

1. Reinhold Niebuhr, *Reflections on the End of an Era* (New York: Scribner, 1934), especially chapter 5.

2. Reinhold Niebuhr, *Moral Man and Immoral Society* (New York: Scribner, 1932), xi.

3. Ibid., 3–4.

4. The source of both the lexical history and the quotation is the *Oxford English Dictionary*, 2nd ed. (1989).

5. In *Liberalism* (1911), the classic essay on the British idea, L. T. Hobhouse ties liberalism to the modern West's antipathy toward power: "The modern State accordingly starts from the basis of an authoritarian order, and the protest against that order, a protest religious, political, economic, social, and ethical, is the historic beginning of Liberalism. Thus Liberalism appears at first as a criticism, sometimes even as a destructive and revolutionary criticism. Its negative aspect is for centuries foremost. Its business seems to be not so much to build up as to pull down, to remove obstacles which block human progress,

rather than to point the positive goal of endeavour or fashion the fabric of civilization. It finds humanity oppressed, and would set it free." Evidently, political liberalism's negative attitude toward the authoritarian state derives from the Enlightenment, and notably British, conviction that the positive element in the "fabric of civilization" is the endeavoring individual who, taken as the essential feature of humanity, must be set free. Hobhouse, *Liberalism* (London: Williams and Norgate, 1911), 10.

6. Jefferson, *Summary of the Rights of British America* (1774), in *Thomas Jefferson, Writings*, ed. Merrill D. Peterson (New York: Library of America, 1984), 105.

7. See Theda Skocpol, *Protecting Soldiers and Mothers: The Political Origins of Social Policy in the United States* (Cambridge: Harvard University Press, 1992); compare W. E. B. Du Bois, *Black Reconstruction in America* (1935; New York: Atheneum, 1992).

8. Walter Russell Mead, *Mortal Splendor* (Boston: Houghton Mifflin, 1987), 34–35. Also see George Lakoff, *Moral Politics: How Liberals and Conservatives Think* (Chicago: University of Chicago Press, 2002).

9. Alan Wolfe, *The Future of Liberalism* (New York: Knopf, 2009), 3–29 and throughout.

10. Niebuhr, *Moral Man*, 33.

11. The lectures were presented at Colgate-Rochester Divinity School in 1934 and published the following year as *An Interpretation of Christian Ethics* (New York: Harper and Brothers, 1935); quotation from 13.

12. Charles C. Brown, *Niebuhr and His Age: Reinhold Niebuhr's Prophetic Role and Legacy*, 2nd ed. (Harrisburg, Pa.: Trinity Press International, 2002), 38–41. Brown attributes the change to a personal encounter with Emil Brunner and a serious reading of Karl Barth.

13. Fordism is jargon for Henry Ford's methods for streamlining the relations of industrial production, including the relation of workers to the factory and wage structure. The method was based on Frederick Winslow Taylor's *Principles of Scientific Management* (1911) and thus is often called Taylorism.

14. Niebuhr, *Moral Man*, 9.

15. Ibid., 14–15.

16. Weber's idea of modern societies was that they were organized, if that is the word, into distinct but overlapping spheres. *The Protestant Ethic and the Spirit of Capitalism*, for example, was a study of the way ethical ideas migrated from the religious sphere to the economic as capitalism came to dominate the social order.

17. Niebuhr, *Moral Man*, 89.

18. Ibid., 83–84.

19. Ibid., 95.

20. Ibid., 108.

21. Ibid., 71.

22. Ibid., 81.

23. The word, of course, is *seminary*. Thanks to Melvin Mattocks for the quotation from a neighborhood preacher of his acquaintance; and for his deep laughter every time he tells the story.

24. Reinhold Niebuhr, "Mystery and Meaning," in *The Essential Reinhold Niebuhr*, ed. Robert McAfee Brown (New Haven: Yale University Press, 1986), 238.

25. Paul Tillich, "The Protestant Principle," *The Protestant Era* (Chicago: University of Chicago Press, 1948), chapter 11.

26. Classically, the core Protestant doctrines have been summarized as the "five solas," where *sola* is a play on the Latin word for alone; hence, salvation is understood as available by: 1) scripture alone, 2) faith alone, 3) grace alone, 4) Christ alone, or 5) God alone. The enduring differences from non-Protestant traditions, such as Roman and Greek Christianities, is that nowhere on the list is mention made of either the Church and its sacraments or of the ordained priest.

27. Reinhold Niebuhr, *Reflections on the End of an Era*, 296.

28. Reinhold Niebuhr, *Leaves from the Notebook of a Tamed Cynic* (Chicago: Willett, Clark, and Colby, 1929), 87.

29. Reinhold Niebuhr, *Nature and Destiny of Man* (New York: Scribner, 1949), 2: 185–86.

30. I heard this story for the first time in a telecast of Clinton's speech to the U.K. Labour Party's annual congress in, as I recall, 1998, and

heard it a number of times thereafter. The idea has since become Democratic Party dogma in the United States.

31. Richard Wightman Fox, *Reinhold Niebuhr: A Biography* (New York: Pantheon, 1985), 200.

32. As in many other factual (as opposed to interpretative) matters. Richard Fox's *Reinhold Niebuhr* (chapter 10) is the most reliable and helpful source. In fact, on the question of Niebuhr's political realism (and with the exception of Donald Meyer's classic work, *The Protestant Search for Political Realism* [Berkeley: University of California Press, 1960]), it is remarkable that most essays and other books on Niebuhr's politics are largely silent on this crucial period in his coming to political maturity. I am especially indebted to both of these books and to Meyer for personal comments he has made.

33. Reinhold Niebuhr, "America's Moral and Spiritual Resources," *World Crisis and American Responsibility* (New York: Association Press, 1958), 31.

34. Reinhold Niebuhr, "Augustine's Political Realism," *Christian Realism and Political Problems* (New York: Scribner, 1953), 126.

35. Reinhold Niebuhr, "The Hazards and the Difficulties of the Christian Ministry," *Justice and Mercy*, ed. Ursula M. Niebuhr (New York: Harper and Row, 1974), 132, 136.

36. Tillich, *The Protestant Era*, 163; emphasis added.

37. Ibid., 176.

38. Niebuhr, "Mystery and Meaning," 249.

39. Niebuhr, *Interpretation of Christian Ethics*, 13.

40. Niebuhr, *Moral Man*, 231.

41. Reinhold Niebuhr, "Innocent Nation in an Innocent World," *The Irony of American History* (New York: Scribner, 1952), 29.

42. There are many versions of these theories of power and its workings. Among the earliest and most influential is Max Horkheimer and Theodor Adorno, *Dialectic of Enlightenment*, trans. Edmund Jephcott (1944; Stanford: Stanford University Press, 2002); and in the same tradition: Herbert Marcuse, *One Dimensional Man* (Boston: Beacon, 1964). The most important departure from these approaches would be

Foucault's power/knowledge concept that emphasizes subjugation of the subject, most fully worked out in *The History of Sexuality*, vol. 1, trans. Robert Hurley (1976; New York: Random House, 1978). Foucault was somewhat influenced by his teacher Louis Althusser, whose "Ideology and the Ideological State Apparatus in Lenin and Philosophy," trans. Ben Brewster, *Monthly Review* (1971 [1969]), is widely read.

43. He did, however, have a clue in his idea of psychic power at work in nonviolence force.

44. Martin Luther King, Jr., "Pilgrimage to Non-Violence," in *The Essential Writings and Speeches of Martin Luther King, Jr.*, ed. James M. Washington (San Francisco: HarperSanFrancisco, 1986), 36.

45. Taylor Branch, *Parting the Waters: America in the King Years, 1954–63* (New York: Simon and Schuster, 1988), 87.

46. Niebuhr, *Moral Man*, 248.

47. Martin Luther King, Jr., "The Power of Nonviolence," in *Essential Writings and Speeches*, 12; emphasis added.

48. See Niebuhr, *Moral Man*, 242.

49. Mahatma Gandhi, *Last Phase* (1958), 2: 65, http://www.mkgandhi.org/gquots1.htm.

CHAPTER FOUR:
SIN, SELF, AND SOCIETY

1. A good account of the circumstances of the hiring and of Union at the time is in Richard Wightman Fox, *Reinhold Niebuhr: A Biography* (New York: Pantheon, 1985), 104–7.

2. For more details on Niebuhr's transition to Union and his intellectual development in the 1930s, see the ever-reliable Charles C. Brown, *Niebuhr and His Age: Reinhold Niebuhr's Prophetic Role and Legacy*, 2nd ed. (Harrisburg, Pa.: Trinity Press International, 2002), chapter 3.

3. The words here are mine, but the ideas are ones that Niebuhr was already developing in the 1930s in *Reflections on the End of an Era* (1934), *Beyond Tragedy* (1937), and *Christianity and Power Politics*

(1940). They would come to fruition in *The Irony of American History* (1952), about which more to come.

4. It was the challenge of Brunner's and Barth's neo-orthodoxies that prompted Niebuhr's scholarly change of heart; see Brown, *Niebuhr and His Age*, 38–39. Union had also welcomed the German pastor Dietrich Bonhoeffer (who declined a post at Union to return to Nazi Germany and his martyrdom) and Paul Tillich (who fled Germany for a position at Union in 1933). Niebuhr taught Bonhoeffer and befriended Tillich, neither of whom was as influential as the Swiss theologians.

5. Barth's international scholarly influence was already considerable by the 1920s. Some went so far as to label him the greatest of all modern theologians—a claim based largely on the originality of Barth's revised second edition of his *Epistle to the Romans* (1992), a commentary on St. Paul's most theological letter.

6. *Nature and Destiny of Man* was published in two volumes: volume 1, *Human Nature*, in 1941, and volume 2, *Human Destiny*, in 1943. Citations are from the later one-volume publication: Reinhold Niebuhr, *Nature and Destiny of Man* (New York: Scribner, 1949). Unfortunately, the combined volume keeps the original separate paginations for the two volumes. So to distinguish the two, I will use the shorthand *NDM* 1: 236–37 (the present citation) for references to the 1941 volume 1 and *NDM* 2 followed by page numbers for references to the 1943 second volume.

7. *NDM* 1: 228–29.

8. Reinhold Niebuhr, *An Interpretation of Christian Ethics* (New York: Harper and Brothers, 1934), originated as the 1934 Rauschenbusch Lectures at the Colgate-Rochester Divinity School.

9. Even more impressive in a way are the recorded lectures he gave at Union *after* his stroke in 1952. He worked, it seems, from notes. Still, he spoke as the preacher he had long been and was able to quote passages from Scripture and long texts from the classical texts with a fluency that only an agile mind could exhibit.

10. Elisabeth Sifton, *The Serenity Prayer* (New York: Norton, 2003).

11. Brown, *Niebuhr and His Age*, 71.

12. Jacques Lacan, "The Mirror Stage as Formative of the *I* as Revealed in Psychoanalytic Experience," in *Écrits: A Selection*, trans. Bruce Fink (New York: Norton, 2002), 75–81.

13. *NDM* 2: 244.

14. Ibid., 1: 14.

15. In this Niebuhr relies heavily on Søren Kierkegaard's *Concept of Dread*, which he originally read in German translation from the Danish and thus uses *anxiety* in place of *dread*—same idea. Also important here is Augustine. See *NDM* 1, "Man as Sinner" (chapter 7).

16. Ibid., 1: 182

17. This is the classic statement of the modern idea of the social self. Niebuhr was thoroughly familiar with the writings of William James. The exact wording of the famous line is "Properly speaking, a man has as many selves as there are individuals who recognize him and carry an image of him in their mind." James, *Principles of Psychology* (1898; Cambridge: Harvard University Press, 1989), 281–82.

18. *NDM* 1: 208–9.

19. See ibid., 1: 208–19.

20. Years later, in "Faith and Empirical Method in Modern Realism," an essay introducing *Christian Realism and Political Problems* (New York: Scribner, 1953) Niebuhr expanded on his method in a way that both affirms the importance of the Christian tradition to politics and recognizes the limits thereof. This collection, some twenty years after *Reflections on the End of an Era*, is a vastly more sophisticated account of global politics, one that puts the Cold War at the center of his concerns. Also, included in this collection is Niebuhr's "Augustine and Political Realism," which had originally been a Frances Carroll Memorial Lecture at Columbia. This relatively short essay, in addition to being a perfect illustration of Niebuhr's method, is his most direct and complete exposition of Augustine's contribution to political realism—a contribution that had been crucial to Niebuhr's theory of human destiny in *Nature and Destiny of Man* a decade earlier.

21. This, in effect, reflects the two sides of Niebuhr's original church training in the Evangelical and Reformed churches—on the one hand,

reformed Protestantism was deterministic; evangelical was optimistic, thus vulnerable to America's liberal ideas of freedom.

22. Reinhold Niebuhr, *Reflections on the End of an Era* (New York: Scribner, 1934), 4.

23. These are symbolic dates, of course. Just as Rome's decline started long before the sack of Rome, so Luther had been studying Paul well before his famous public challenge to the pope.

24. Charles Norris Cochrane, *Christianity and Classical Culture: A Study of Thought and Action from Augustus to Augustine* (Oxford: Oxford University Press, 1940), 456.

25. Augustine, *De Trinitate* [On the Trinity], trans. Edmund Hill (New York: New City, 1991), 298 (10: 17–18); emphasis added.

26. Oddly, a leading philosopher of the history of the self misreads Augustine as almost wholly Platonic in his thinking: Charles Taylor, *Sources of the Self* (Cambridge: Harvard University Press, 1989), chapter 7.

27. Niebuhr refers to these lines in *NDM* 2: 108, where he reprises the long discussion of sin in *NDM* 1 (chapters 7–10).

28. Reinhold Niebuhr, "Ethics of Augustine," audio recording of a lecture at Union Theological Seminary in New York, Reinhold Niebuhr Audio Collection, CD N665 40, 1960 (Union Theological Seminary and Presbyterian School of Christian Education, Richmond, Va.).

29. Hayden White, *Metahistory: The Historical Imagination in Nineteenth-Century Europe* (Baltimore: Johns Hopkins University Press, 1975).

30. Augustine, *Concerning the City of God against the Pagans*, trans. Henry Bettenson (1972) (New York: Penguin Classics, 2003), preface to book 1; ellipsis indicates a lengthy omission.

31. Ibid., book 4, chapter 5.

32. Ibid., chapter 4; the pirate story is attributed to Cicero, *De Re Publica*, 3, 14, 24.

33. Cochrane, *Christianity and Classical Culture*, 516, 513.

34. *NDM* 2: 4–5; emphasis added; ellipsis indicates a lengthy omission.

35. Brown, *Niebuhr and His Age*, 15–16.

36. For a pungent summary of the varieties of falsely messianic cultures, see *NDM* 2: 306, notes 9 and 10.

37. "Special providence" is an expression borrowed from Walter Russell Mead's *Special Providence* (New York: Knopf, 2001); Mead in turn borrowed it from Otto von Bismarck (who may have gotten it from Shakespeare). Mead may not approve of this usage, though it is evident that he approves of Niebuhr, at least the Niebuhr of *Moral Man* (see Mead, *God and Gold: Britain, America, and the Making of the Modern World* [New York: Vintage, 2007]).

38. *NDM* 2: 305.

39. Ibid., 321.

40. Reinhold Niebuhr, *The Children of Light and the Children of Darkness: A Vindication of Democracy and a Critique of Its Traditional Defense* (New York: Scribner, 1944), 1.

41. Ibid., 11, 9.

42. One of Niebuhr's most astute former students and recent interpreters, Langdon Gilkey, makes the common error of suggesting that Niebuhr should have been considered neoliberal instead of neo-orthodox; Gilkey, *On Niebuhr* (Chicago: University of Chicago Press, 2001), 27–28. The mistake is a typically American confusion of liberalism with a brand of leftist politics. Neoliberalism, instead, even now in America, is a renewal of market principles on a global scale—a policy attitude that Niebuhr would have immediately rejected. See, in particular, *Reflections on the End of an Era*. Niebuhr was both more European in his understanding of liberal values as market-oriented individualism and, given his background in the German Protestant traditions, unafraid of the term *orthodox*.

CHAPTER FIVE: NATIONS,
GLOBAL POLITICS, AND
RELIGION

1. Reinhold Niebuhr, "Intellectual Autobiography," in *Reinhold Niebuhr: His Religious, Social, and Political Thought*, ed. Charles W.

Kegley and Robert W. Bretall (New York: Macmillan, 1956), 3–4. Mark Hopkins was a nineteenth-century educator of such renown that President James A. Garfield is said to have delivered the line that Niebuhr here invokes.

2. Again, and again, Augustine was a pivotal figure in Christian thought and in Niebuhr's own mature intellectual and political position. A brilliant book, still relatively recent, exposes the struggles Augustine himself went through in his understanding of the centrality of the Jewish people to the founding and continuing history of Christianity: Paula Fredriksen, *Augustine and the Jews: A Christian Defense of Jews and Judaism* (New York: Doubleday, 2008).

3. Reinhold Niebuhr, *Nature and Destiny of Man* (New York: Scribner, 1949), 2: 321.

4. Quoted in Richard Wightman Fox, *Reinhold Niebuhr: A Biography* (New York: Pantheon, 1985), 293.

5. On the relationship between classical and ancient empires and globalization see Charles Lemert, Anthony Elliott, Daniel Chaffee, and Eric Hsu, eds., *Globalization: A Reader* (London: Routledge, 2010), especially parts 1 and 2.

6. Reinhold Niebuhr, "Christians and Jews in Western Civilization," in *The Essential Reinhold Niebuhr*, ed. Robert McAfee Brown (New Haven: Yale University Press, 1986), chapter 13.

7. Reinhold Niebuhr, *The Structure of Nations and Empires: A Study of the Recurring Patterns and Problems of the Political Order in Relation to the Unique Problems of the Nuclear Age* (New York: Scribner, 1959), 33.

8. One might say that the European Union is trying to reverse the Westphalian system—an interstate system that favors international community over national authority within territorial boundaries.

9. Late in life, especially in the 1960s, he repeatedly said that in *Moral Man* he had overrated the ability of individuals to outrun their more devious interests and the inability of the social to be just. In the preface to the 1960 edition he clarified his thinking: "The central thesis was, and is, that the Liberal Movement both religious and secular

seemed to be unconscious of the basic difference between the morality of individuals and the morality of collectives, whether races, classes or nations. This difference ought not to make for a moral cynicism, that is, the belief that the collective must follow its own interests."

10. See Jürgen Habermas, *Legitimation Crisis*, trans. Thomas McCarthy (Boston: Beacon, 1975). Habermas, who has changed his position on many of his early ideas, continues to apply the legitimation crisis, most interestingly to the dilemma of postnational states and the European Union: Habermas, *The Divided West*, ed. and trans. Ciaran Cronin (Cambridge: Polity, 2006), 177–79.

11. Charles Brown is particularly good on this point: *Niebuhr and His Age: Reinhold Niebuhr's Prophetic Role and Legacy*, 2nd ed. (Harrisburg, Pa.: Trinity Press International, 2002), 165–66. But see Niebuhr, *Christian Realism and Political Problems* (New York: Scribner, 1953), chapter 5.

12. Reinhold Niebuhr, "Two Aspects of Our Tumultuous Age" and "Man and Society," recorded speeches, 1960, Reinhold Niebuhr Audio Collection, CD N665 57–58 (Union Theological Seminary and Presbyterian School of Christian Education, Richmond, Va.).

13. The challenge was put to me some years ago, almost in passing, by Jerry G. Watts. I have thought of it ever since and come to think the answer I here propose is correct but also, in many ways, the key to appreciating Niebuhr and his times and their importance to ours.

14. Reinhold Niebuhr, "Man and Society" radio talk, 1960, Niebuhr Audio Collection, CD N665 58. The name of the expert is indicated on the disk from which the interested can judge the accuracy of my characterization. I choose not to use the name here because he, having died in 2008, is not here to defend himself, and in any case the Cold War years were ones of terrible confusion when men were stilted and history hard to figure.

15. In this situation, and others, Niebuhr did avow that America was a Christian nation, as he did in many talks and writings of these years. But, at least in my view, the stance was not crass so much as thoughtful. Some, I do not doubt, would find the position objectionable by any

measure. But in the throes of Cold War, if Niebuhr hedged a bit his long-standing appreciation of the limits of worldly Christianity, the hedge was always, I think, in the context of again his Christian theory of history as always under the prospect of an unanticipated interruption from the outside—under, that is, the judgment of a messiah.

16. On the United States and the USSR as civil religions, see *Structure of Nations and Empires*, among many other places, including the "Man and Society" radio talk.

17. The precise number turns out to be disputed. Some sources, including Niebuhr, put the U.S. figure as high as 60 percent of the global manufacturing output. Another puts it at 40 percent in 1945; many say at least 50 percent. In either case, the complete destruction of the industrial infrastructure among the Axis nations and the relative exhaustion of manufacturing in Great Britain left the United States as the sole industrialized nation untouched by the war and, in fact, strengthened by the war effort. If one takes 50 percent as the modal number, then perspective is gained by knowing that sixty years later, in 2005, when the American economy remained the world's most productive by volume and rate, the U.S. gross domestic product was half of the 1945 level—little more than 25 percent. All this is figurative in the sense that I am mixing and matching measures and exact years, but the rough idea holds.

18. Joseph Stalin, "Interview with Pravda on Churchill," *New York Times*, March 14, 1946.

19. Reinhold Niebuhr, "The Two Imperial Nations of Today," in *Structure of Nations and Empires*, 10; note that where Stalin had used *motherland* in reference to Russia, Niebuhr used *fatherland*, a curious, if irrelevant, nuance revealing, perhaps, Niebuhr's deeper suspicion of the ability of the Soviets to hold maternal virtues. Niebuhr admired his authoritarian father, who died young; he doted on his mother, who was his partner in the Detroit parish and for whom he provided a home in New York.

20. Reinhold Niebuhr, "Individual and Collective Destinies in the Contemporary Situation," in *The Self and the Dramas of History* (New York: Scribner, 1955), 217.

21. Reinhold Niebuhr, "Why Is Communism So Evil?" in *Christian Realism and Political Problems* (New York: Scribner, 1953), 33–42; but in the same book see "Foreign Policy of American Conservatism and Liberalism," where he writes: "The liberal creed in its various facets is characteristic of the ethics of the bourgeois class; and . . . a weapon in its fight against the aristocracy as it sought to disintegrate the old, feudal society in favor of a society in which the individual would have fewer restrains upon his initiative" (55).

22. A still valuable documentation of the nature of American anti-Asian racisms in World War II is Ruth Benedict, *The Chrysanthemum and the Sword: Patterns of Japanese Culture* (Boston: Houghton Mifflin, 1946).

23. George Kennan, "Long Telegram [on the Soviet Outlook]," February 22, 1946. The famous telegram is captioned (and written) in the manner of an official State Department telegram: "861.00/2-2246: Telegram / *Chargé in the Soviet Union (Kennan) to the Secretary of State* / SECRET / Moscow, February 22, 1946–9 P.M. [Received February 22–3:52 P.M.]." The telegram came to 5,363 words—long.

24. Reinhold Niebuhr, "Innocent Nation in an Innocent World," in *The Irony of American History* (New York: Scribner, 1952), 35.

25. On Tocqueville and the history of the concept see Anthony Elliott and Charles Lemert, *The New Individualism: The Emotional Costs of Globalization* (London: Routledge, 2006).

26. Niebuhr, *Irony of American History*, 28.

27. Figures are for 2005 from CIA *Factbook*, U.S. Bureau of Census, http://www.adherents.com, and are summarized reliably in "Protestantism by Country," http://en.wikipedia.org/wiki/Protestantism_by_country.

28. A February 2008 Pew Foundation survey of religious affiliation and social values found that Roman Catholics held positions nearly identical with the national average and no more than a few points off from mainline Protestant churches and, in many cases, evangelical churches. Most astonishing of all, American Catholics had almost exactly the same attitudes as mainline Protestants on abortion rights, America's role in world affairs, and homosexual rights. See Pew Forum

on Religion and Public Life, "U.S. Religious Landscape Survey," February 2008, http://religions.pewforum.org/comparisons#.

29. Among other places, Max Weber, *Economy and Society*, ed. Guenter Roth, trans. Roth et al. (Berkeley: University of California Press, 1978), 58.

30. Niebuhr, *Irony of American History*, 45.

31. Niebuhr, *Structure of Nations and Empires*, 17.

32. *NDM* 2: 18.

33. Reinhold Niebuhr, "The Ironic Situation," in *Irony of American History*, 2–3; also compare the 1953 collection of essays, *Christian Realism and Political Problems*, in which, as in *Irony*, Niebuhr remains somewhat remote from the realities of the Cold War. Some of the essays in both books date to the late 1940s, which may explain the relatively mild language that would be replaced later in the 1950s by a more forceful language which is only occasionally in evidence in these earlier books (as in "Why Is Communism So Evil?" in *Christian Realism*).

34. Niebuhr, *Irony of American History*, 23–24.

35. George Marsden, *Jonathan Edwards: A Life* (New Haven: Yale University Press, 2003).

36. Jonathan Edwards, "Sinners in the Hands of an Angry God" (1741), http://www.jonathan-edwards.org/Sinners.html.

37. Niebuhr, *Irony of American History*, 2.

38. Robert N. Bellah, "Civil Religion in America," *Daedalus: Journal of the American Academy of Arts and Sciences* 96, no. 1 (winter 1967), 1–21.

39. Walter Russell Mead, "God's Country," *Foreign Affairs* 85, no. 5 (September–October 2006), 25.

40. Niebuhr, *Moral Man*, 79.

CHAPTER SIX: POLITICAL RECOVERY AND GLOBALIZATION

1. The 2008 attempt by a Yale archivist to discredit Niebuhr as the author of the Serenity Prayer (see Introduction, note 4) is based in large part on its words occurring much earlier than 1943, the date Elisabeth

Sifton, among others, identified for Niebuhr's authorship. What a pure archival search cannot possibly account for is that speakers of all kinds, and preachers in particular, work and rework their words, sometimes for years, before (if at all) committing them to paper. This is especially true of Niebuhr, who seldom used written texts in his religious work. See Laurie Goodstein, "Serenity Prayer Stirs up Doubt on Who Wrote It," *New York Times*, July 11, 2008. For the story of the German who claimed authorship see Elisabeth Sifton, *The Serenity Prayer* (New York: Norton, 2003), chapter 7.

2. The date is said to be the first day of the permanent sobriety of Doctor Bob, one of the AA movement's cofounders; see *Alcoholics Anonymous*, 3rd ed. (New York: Alcoholics Anonymous World Services, 1976), 171.

3. The Oxford Group should be distinguished from the formal Oxford movement in the Anglican Church. The former was a Christian-based movement that led to a variety of social outcomes, including AA. The latter was a high church movement meant to associate conservative Anglican churches with the Catholic Church.

4. In this, the most telling instance is the influence of William James and, indirectly, Carl Jung on Bill W(ilson), the cofounder of AA—in particular on the principle of hitting bottom. See Robert D. Richardson, *William James, in the Maelstrom of Modernism* (Boston: Houghton Mifflin, 2007), 531*n*16, for Wilson's view that "James, though long in his grave, had been a founder of Alcoholics Anonymous." In James you find this principle most eloquently articulated in the conclusion to *Varieties of Religious Experience*, his 1901–2 Gifford lectures.

5. One of the reasons these steps are so difficult is that, for many, the thought of turning one's life over to a god, any god, is inconceivable, even with the proviso "God *as we understood Him.*" This emendation is one of the ways the twelve-step tradition, since its inception in 1935, has adjusted its program to the realities of addiction by softening the strong religious principle of "God" into a mysterious higher power. Yet the religious element seems to be inescapable. The program works only when drunks and other addicts admit that they are powerless to control

their addictions, which in turn requires a turn to a higher power that will "restore us to sanity." What makes the program work, when it works, for however long, is that it is rooted in local communities of people who, in principle, never learn each other's full names, who come together regularly to speak in common terms. "*We* admitted *we* were powerless over alcohol—that *our* lives had become unmanageable." If others can say these words, even when an individual cannot, then the effect is to create the sense of common bond that, one supposes, becomes the higher power for those without a working god.

6. Sifton, *Serenity Prayer*, 292–93. Also, the longer version omitted by AA:

Living one day at a time,
Enjoying one moment at a time,
Accepting hardship as a pathway to peace,
Taking, as Jesus did,
This sinful world as it is,
Not as I would have it,
Trusting that You will make all things right,
If I surrender to Your will,
So that I may be reasonably happy in this life,
And supremely happy with You forever in the next.

7. Ibid., 293.

8. Reinhold Niebuhr, "A View of Life from the Sidelines," in *The Essential Reinhold Niebuhr*, ed. Robert McAfee Brown (New Haven: Yale University Press, 1986), 254.

9. Reinhold Niebuhr, *Nature and Destiny of Man* (New York: Scribner, 1949), 2: 321; also note that the Gifford lectures delivered in 1939 were some four years before the Serenity Prayer was written and contain very nearly the same wording and certainly the same idea. Sifton quotes this line near the end of her book on her father's prayer.

10. On Europe, among others see Anthony Giddens, *Europe in a Global Age* (Cambridge: Polity, 2006), and Timothy Garton Ash, *Free World: America, Europe, and the Surprising Future of the World* (New

York: Random House, 2004). And in respect to economic realities and states of exception see Aihwa Ong, *Neoliberalism as Exception* (Durham, N.C.: Duke University Press, 2006), and among many others Parag Khanna, *The Second World* (New York: Random House, 2008).

11. Giorgio Agamben, *The Time That Remains: A Commentary on the Letter to the Romans*, trans. Patricia Dailey (2000; Stanford: Stanford University Press, 2005).

12. Giorgio Agamben, *Homo Sacer: Sovereign Power and Bare Life*, trans. Daniel Heller-Roazen (Stanford: Stanford University Press, 1998), 181.

acknowledgments

John Donatich continued to believe in this book even after a few ill-conceived starts. His editorial advice was more than wonderful at every turn. My two editors at Yale University Press helped me immeasurably. Ileene Smith gently forced me to rethink an early draft. Jennifer Banks came into the project after that and provided what is easily the best line-by-line editing I have enjoyed in a long career of book publishing.

The book is dedicated to the memory of the Reverend Joseph C. Williamson, who died in 2008. Joe befriended me during the years of my theological study at Andover Newton Theological School and Harvard Divinity School. Without him in those days I would not have stayed with religious studies and the ministry as long as I did. After I left it all, I lost touch with him as he continued the political and religious work we had shared in the 1960s. He was an Edwards scholar who surely knew his

Niebuhr, about whom we never once had a conversation. Yet when I attended his memorial services in Boston, I learned from others just how much he had lived a life that was as Niebuhrian as any could be—politically engaged, theologically astute, morally committed, and homiletically brilliant.

Index

abolition, 11

Abraham, 147

Abrahamic faiths, 109, 138

acceptance, 209–10

Acts of Apostles, 33

Adams, John, 49, 178, 184

addictions, 193–95, 233–34n5

Adorno, Theodor, 90

Agamben, Giorgio, 204

Alcoholics Anonymous, 193–95

Alexander the Great, 135

allegory, parables as, 37

America. *See* United States

American Century, 142

American Federation of Labor
(AFL), 19

American Friends of German
Freedom, 78

American Left, 79

American Revolution, 80

Americans for Democratic Action
(ADA), 79

Amos (prophet), 138, 146–48

anxiety, 69, 119

Aristotle, 109

arrogance, 41–42, 43, 107, 108

Asia, postwar recovery of, 142, 198

Atheists for Niebuhr, 122

Augustine of Hippo, 126–37, 145,
204; *The City of God,* 129, 132–37,
141; *Confessions,* 129; death of,
140; Niebuhr's *Nature and
Destiny of Man* compared with,
135–37, 139–41; *On the Trinity,*
129, 136; theory of civilizations,
131–37, 142

Augustus, Emperor, 129

automobile industry, 12, 55

Barth, Karl, 35, 104, 110, 112

Bay of Pigs, 163

Bellah, Robert, "Civil Religion in
America," 188–89

Berlin War, 163

Bethel Church, Detroit, 11, 19, 64
Bloom, Harold, 31
Bonhoeffer, Dietrich, 224n4
Bono, 207
Branch, Taylor, 92, 93
Britain: Anglican Christianity in, 183; national unity sought in, 59
Brunner, Emil, 104, 110
Bush, George W., "axis of evil," xii

Calvin, John, 9
Calvinism: discipline of, 8, 25, 108, 174; and Great Awakening, 184; and national religion, 183; and rationalism, 184
capitalism: continuous economic growth in, 51, 209; corporate intimidation in, 48; economic injustices of, 14, 56–57, 207; and exploration for new wealth, 51; and Fordism, 220n13; free markets in, 81; global crisis in, 76, 140; and Great Depression, 45, 53, 58, 125; and greed, 19, 20–21, 54, 61, 73, 76, 89, 154, 175, 209; in individualistic cultures, 51; and the invisible hand, 47; Marxist critique of, 74, 160, 164, 197–98; Niebuhr's crisis of, 135–36; profit motive in, 74, 175; workers exploited in, 73, 74, 89
Castro, Fidel, 168
Catholics: in cities, 8; crucifixes of, 69; populations of, 174; and priestly class, 127
Chamberlain, Neville, 153

Charles the Great, Holy Roman Emperor, 133
Cheney, Dick, 154
China: civil war in, 162, 167–68; Confucian revival in, xiii; Cultural Revolution in, 158, 206; economy of, 200; and Korean War, 167
Chomsky, Noam, 112
Christian Century, 20
Christian Diaspora, 105
Christianity: early and medieval, 111; endurance of, 34; Eucharist in, 34, 128; liberal, 53, 189–90; and perfectionism, 61–62; puritanical thinking in, 9, 108, 109–10; susceptibility to corruption, 124; and world vs. Church, 75
Christianity and Crisis, 78
Christian realism, 25, 43–44, 75, 136–37, 159
church: and immoral society, 61; world vs., 75. See also religion
Churchill, Winston, 27, 170
Church universal, 4
civilization, modern, 20
civil rights, 11, 94–98
Civil War, U.S., 49, 188
Clinton, Bill, 75, 206–7
Cochrane, Charles Norris, 126–27, 128, 136
coercion: of economic greed, 58; of power, 57–58, 59, 60, 88–89; of social groups and states, 47, 57, 58, 59–60, 87, 88–89

Coffin, Henry Sloane, 102

Cold War, 162–72, 190, 203;
    ideology of, 91; and Iron Curtain,
    170; onset of, 142,
    162, 164–65; overview of,
    158; realities of, 150, 161,
    179, 181–82, 187–88; unanswerable
    questions on, 200–203

Columbia University, New York,
    102, 103

Communism, 53; anticommunism
    vs., 79, 162, 166, 171, 187; and Cold
    War, 162, 163, 168; containment of,
    169; nationalism vs., 187; Niebuhr's
    criticism of, 158, 167; and Red
    Scare, 167, 171

communities, 116, 152, 203, 234n5

Confucian revival, xiii

Congregational Church, 10–11

conscience, 62, 83, 84

conservative ideologies, 75

conservatives: American
    Right, 79, 187, 189; liberals vs.,
    52, 75; and power, 143; Tories
    as, 49

Constitution, U.S., 86, 183

corporations: evils of, 16; greed in,
    52, 175; power of, 96

crash of 1929. *See* stock market
    crash

creativity, 154–57

Crevecoeur, Michel de, *Letters from
    an American Farmer,* 178

Crozer Theological Seminary,
    Philadelphia, 92, 93

Cuban missile crisis, 163, 205

Cuban Revolution, 168

Dancy, John C., 21–22

Darius, Emperor, 130

death: dealing with, 118, 119–20, 125,
    161; and despair, 68–69; fear of,
    69, 113, 196; inevitability of, 139

Declaration of Independence, 49, 183

Deists, 182–83, 184

Delta Cooperative Farm, 13

democracy: consent of the governed
    in, 56, 155; have-nots in, 29, 207;
    individual liberties and social
    justice balanced in, 24, 27–29, 51,
    57, 72–75, 81, 95–96, 186; liberal,
    50; and market values, 81; and
    nation-state, 59; Niebuhr's
    vindication of, 140–42; in
    post-World War II world, 142;
    preservation of, 158; rational, 61;
    rise of, 56

Descartes, René, 118

destiny, limits of, 140, 151

Detroit: industrial life in, 24;
    Niebuhr's departure from, 21–22,
    23; Niebuhr's early
    social activism in, 12–14, 24;
    Niebuhr's ministry in, 11,
    19–20, 73

Dexter Avenue Baptist Church,
    Montgomery, 94

Disney, Walt, 21

domination, 176

Douglas, Mary, 112

Du Bois, W. E. B., 93

Durkheim, Émile, 180

Ebenezer Baptist Church, Atlanta, 92

Eddy, Sherwood, 102

Edwards, Jonathan, 184–86; "Sinners in the Hands of an Angry God," 185
Eisenhower, Dwight D., 156
electoral process, as market for votes, 50
Elshtain, Jean Bethke, 213n1
Emancipation Proclamation, 98
Engels, Friedrich, 73
Enlightenment, 176, 182, 185
Erikson, Erik, 170
eschatology, 140, 159, 160
ethics: individual, 55; morality of intentions, 87; and "Ought" vs. "Is," 85, 95; philosophical, 85; social, 24, 63, 85, 91; virtue, 127
Eucharist, 34, 128
Europe: community of, 151–53, 198, 200, 228n8; destructiveness of war in, 151; partitioning of, 205; postwar recovery of, 142, 179–80, 201, 202, 203; socialism in, 177
evangelical, definition, 31
Evangelical and Reformed (E and R) Church, 10
evangelical Protestantism: and Calvin's teaching, 9; and Lutheranism, 9; meaning of, 31–32, 40; and Niebuhr's preaching, 35–36, 67–68; and the Reformation, 34; and secular humanity, 122; and Social Gospel movement, 18; in twenty-first century, 189
evangelical Right, xiii–xiv, 189
Evangelical Synod of North America, 4, 8, 9–10

evangelist, reborn, 67–68
evil: of capitalist classes, 57, 73; children of darkness, 141–42; in the face of the other, 97; good vs., 26, 38, 39, 43, 106–7; and hell, 185; human rights movement vs., 176; of political figures, 143; and sin, 41; theory of, 25; in war, 78
Ezekiel (prophet), 147, 148

faith, 69–70; of the believer, 39–40, 68, 71, 126, 221n26; in faith, 82, 182; paradox of, 72, 84; and the Protestant principle, 83–84
fascism, 77, 90; democracy vs., 142, 158, 177; and national immorality, 58, 141; nationalism as false prophetic voice in, 138; and World War II, 112, 113, 158
Federalist Papers, 183
Ford, Henry, 12, 19, 24, 53, 54, 55, 76
Fordism, 220n13
Ford Motor Company, 12
Fosdick, Harry Emerson, 102
Foucault, Michel, 90, 176
France, Socialists in, 50
Francis of Assisi, Saint, 193
Frankfurter, Felix, 149
Franklin, Benjamin, 178, 182, 186
Freedman's Bureau, 49
Freud, Sigmund, 180
fundamentalists, 67, 189

Galbraith, John Kenneth, 79, 170
Gandhi, Mohandas K. "Mahatma," 95–97; and King, 92, 94, 95–96;

and *Satyagraha* (soul-force), 96–97

German immigrant communities, 8

Germany: economic retributions on, 58; Frankfurt School in, 90; and Holocaust, 104, 158; Nazi party in, 25, 46, 84, 90; postwar recovery of, 201; and Versailles Treaty, 20

Gettysburg Address (Lincoln), 188

Gifford Lectures on Natural Theology, 111–12, 234n9

Gladden, Washington, 17; "O Master, Let Me Walk with Thee," 18, 216n16

globalization, 150, 187, 200, 206–9; interrelatedness in, 210; and isolation, 208; and permanent economic growth, 209; possibility in, 207–8; and wealth gap, 207

God: literal words of, 67; love of, 34–35; media evocation of, 86; need for, 195; paradoxical nature of, 72; power of, 185; salvation through, 221n26; in twelve-step programs, 195, 233–34n5; will of, on earth, 182

Goffman, Erving, 170

Gospel, The, 32–35, 38, 39–40, 42, 55

Gospel of Good News, 33, 39–40

gospels, 32–33

grace: experience of, 32; salvation by, 175, 221n26

Great Awakening, 184, 185

Great Depression, 12, 86, 106; and capitalism, 45, 53, 58, 125; as

historical crisis, 125, 190; and postwar realities, 76; and Roosevelt, 26–27, 54, 177

Greco-Roman philosophy, 132

Greek philosophy, 109, 111, 127, 140

group egotism, 120

groups, morality of, 46–47

Habermas, Jürgen, 155

Hamilton, Alexander, 49

Han Dynasties, 130

Hebrew prophets, 55

Hegel, G. W. F., 123

Heimert, Alan, xvi

Heschel, Rabbi Abraham, 149

higher power, need for, 195

historical progress, absolutistic theory of, 159

history, 128–29; Augustine's theory of, 132–35; basic truth of, 210; biblical view of, 204; consequences of, 198; creativity of, 139; cyclical theory of, 131–32; deterministic theory of, 203; discovery of, 127; distortion of, 180–81; End of, 140, 159–60, 203; eventuality of, 160; evidence of, 123–26; incompleteness of, 139–40, 160; Niebuhr's theories of, 123–26, 139, 159–60, 190, 203–4; Paul's theory of, 129; White's levels in writing of, 131–32

Hitler, Adolf, 46, 86, 90, 104, 153–54, 158, 163

Hobbes, Thomas, 176

Hobhouse, L. T., *Liberalism,* 219–20n5

Holocaust, 78, 104, 158

Holy Roman Empire, 34, 153

Hopkins, Mark, 146

Horkheimer, Max, 90

Hosea (prophet), 147, 148

human beings: animal instincts of, 113–14, 117; community of, 116; destiny of, 125–26; as historical species, 139–40; language of, 114; nature of, 113, 115, 117; needs and wants of, 117, 118; self-consciousness of, 114–15, 116–17, 118–20; social selves of, 119–21; thoughtlessness of, 115–16, 117

human frailty, 44

human freedom, 122, 123–24

human life, central dilemma of, 70

human rights movement, 176

human spirit: homelessness of, 117–18; Niebuhr's theory of, 185; power of, 42

human suffering, 85–86

humility, 160

hypocrisy, 60, 61, 62, 87, 96, 98

individualism, 62, 72, 81; and freedom, 175; and liberalism, 52, 169, 173; moral, 16, 82–83, 174–75, 210; in postwar U.S., 171–74; and Protestantism, 173–76; psychology of, 126–27

individuals vs. societies, 120–21, 151, 154–57, 185, 210

industrialization, 20–21, 24, 55, 75, 105, 175

infants, mirror stage of, 114–15

Iraq, 199

Iron Curtain, 170

irony, parables as, 37–38, 42

Isaiah, Book of, 147, 149

Islam: puritanical thinking in, 109; radical, xiii, xiv

Israel: founding of, 79, 149–50, 151; nationalism of, 138; Niebuhr as friend to, 146, 150; prophets of, 146–48, 204

James, William, 119, 195, 233n4; *Varieties of Religious Experience,* 111

Japan: postwar recovery of, 201; and World War II, 168

Jefferson, Thomas, 49, 178, 182–83, 184

Jeremiah (prophet), 147

Jerusalem, 150

Jesus of Nazareth, 147; false Christ, 139; Great Commandment of, 62; as messiah, 128, 138; salvation through, 127, 221n26; second coming of, 40, 137–38; story of, 31–32, 33; the Way, 40

Jewish Theological Seminary, New York, 103, 150

Jews: anti-Semitism, 90; Diaspora of, 150; and Holocaust, 78, 104; national homeland for, 78, 79

John, Gospel According to, 32–33

Johnson, Lyndon B., 75

joy, 210–11

Judaism: puritanical thinking in, 109; rabbi as teacher, 67

Julius Caesar, 129
Jung, Carl, 233n4
justice, 61, 98, 148, 151, 176

Kennan, George, 169–70, 171, 187
Kennedy, John F., 75, 163, 205
Khrushchev, Nikita, 157, 165, 205
Kierkegaard, Søren, 119; *Sickness Unto Death,* 68
King, Rev. Martin Luther, Jr., 92–98; and civil rights movement, 94–98; Gandhi's influence on, 92, 94, 95–96; influence of, 94; Niebuhr's influence on, 92, 94, 96, 97; and nonviolence, 92, 94–96; as public speaker, 93; studies of, 92, 93, 94
King, Rev. Martin Luther, Sr., 92, 93
Kissinger, Henry A., 159
knowledge, limits of, 148
Korean War, 162, 167, 168, 180

Labour Party (Britain), 50
Lacan, Jacques, 114
laissez faire, 52
language, 114
large structural forces, amoral power of, xv–xvi
Leftist politics, 26, 50
liberal: conservative vs., 52, 75; as "free," 48; modern use of the term, 50
liberal Christianity, 53, 189–90
liberal democracies, 50
liberalism, 11, 90; and the art of the possible, 55; definitions of, 50–51;

dilemma of, 75; and economic policies, 50; and electoral politics, 75; and the Founders, 49; and individualism, 52, 169, 173; individual vs. state rights, 52, 54; and Leftist politics, 50, 79, 227n42; and market values, 81; and modern values, 54–55, 81; neoliberalism, 206; Niebuhr's criticism of, 94, 112, 139, 159, 167; Niebuhr's use of the term, 48–52, 124; nineteenth-century, 76; and power, 47–48, 52–53, 74, 143, 172; religious, 47, 55; and Social Gospel, 24, 53, 54; and socialism, 91; and suspicion of power, 49; in twenty-first century, 143; and utopian ideals, 20, 56, 125, 160
Liberal Party (Britain), 50
liberal realism, 11
liberty: Christian, 8; individual, 49
life is short, 38
Lincoln, Abraham, 98, 132, 177, 188
Lippmann, Walter, xvi
love: of God, 34–35; individual ethic of, 55, 86; powerlessness of, 77, 98; and religion, 61–62
Lowell, Robert, 188
Luke, Gospel According to, 32–33
Luther, Martin, 9, 62, 126, 204; *Treatise on Christian Liberty,* 72
Lutheranism: on Christian liberty, 8; conservatism of, 9; in Midwest, 8; and paradox of faith, 72

MacArthur, Douglas, 167

Macedonian Empire, 130

Machiavelli, Niccolò, 77

Madison, James, 49, 80, 178, 183

man: as creature and creator, 43–44; Niebuhr's definition of, 124; ungendered use of term, 42, 110

manifest destiny, 181

Mao Tse-tung, 158, 162, 168, 206

market freedoms, 81

Mark, Gospel According to, 32–33

Marx, Karl, 180; on capitalism, 57, 73, 197–98; and Engels, *Communist Manifesto,* 74; on religion as opiate, 197; on state power, 61

Marxism, 73–74; and capitalism, 74, 160, 164, 197–98; Kennan's idea of, 170; and liberalism, 124; Niebuhr's critique of, 53, 89–90, 91, 95, 126, 139, 159; Niebuhr's passing interest in, 56

mass media, 48, 86, 154, 155–56

Matthew, Gospel According to, 32–33

McCarthy, Joseph, 158, 167, 169, 187

Mead, Walter Russell, 50; "God's Country," 189

meaning, search for, 115

memory, and self, 127–28

Mennonites, 8

messianism: nationalistic, 138–39, 180, 181, 182, 183, 185, 187, 203, 204; prophetic, 185, 204

metaphor, parables as, 37

Middle East, global conflict in, 149–51

Mill, John Stuart, 49

Miller, Perry, 181

mind-body dualism, 127

modernity: culture of, 53, 86, 132, 139; and the End of history, 140; Niebuhr's criticism of, 139

Montgomery, Alabama, civil rights movement in, 94, 95, 97

moral cynicism, 229n9

Moral Man and Immoral Society (Niebuhr), 14, 45–48, 103, 157; on the immorality of society, 47, 59–60; on individual vs. group behavior, 46–47, 72–75, 79, 88, 120–21; and King and Gandhi, 92–93, 94–95, 96–97, 98; on liberalism, 47, 48, 52–53, 54–55, 90, 94, 112; "The Morality of Nations" essay in, 91; and Niebuhr's ideological transformation, 53–55, 62–63, 76, 79–80, 89, 112; on power and coercion, 47–48, 52–53, 55–61, 73, 74, 75, 88–90, 98–99; "The Preservation of Moral Values in Politics" essay in, 91–92, 94; and the pulpit, 86–87, 89; and realism, 47, 55, 75–78, 136–37; and social ethics, 63, 85, 87, 90–92, 95, 99, 112, 148

moral principles, absolutizing, 61–62

national identity, 170–72

nationalism: vs. communism, 187; as false prophetic voice, 138–39, 169; history distorted in, 180–81,

182; messianistic, 138–39, 180, 181, 182, 183, 185, 187, 203, 204

nation-state. *See* state

Nazi Party, 25, 46, 84, 90

neoliberalism, 206, 227n42

New Deal, 54

Niebuhr, Gustav (father), 3–4; death of, 202; and Evangelical Synod, 4, 8, 9; and his family, 7–8; influence on his son, 3–4, 7, 105, 146, 147, 161, 202, 230n19

Niebuhr, Gustav (grand-nephew), 6

Niebuhr, Hulda (sister), 5

Niebuhr, Lydia (mother), 3, 7

Niebuhr, Reinhold: at Bethel Church, Detroit, 11, 19, 64; birth of, 1–3; childhood of, 3, 5, 7, 105, 138, 161; death of, xiii, 14; energy of, 14; faith of, 29, 31, 68, 75; family background of, 3, 6–7; Gifford Lectures of, 111–12, 234n9; and his father, 3–4, 7, 105, 146, 147, 161, 202, 230n19; and history, 123–26, 139; influence of, 19–20, 22, 23, 30, 64, 91–98, 112, 186; influences on, 145–46, 159, 166, 204; journal of, 15, 16; language used by, 48; lectures delivered by, 53, 161–62; neo-orthodox views of, 41, 54, 124, 227n42; and nonviolent activism, 95–98; organizations supported by, 13, 78; patience of, 13–14, 162; as preacher, 29–31, 32, 35–36, 63–64, 102, 111, 122; reputation of, 23, 102–3, 112; revised thinking of, 76, 77, 79–80, 106–7, 216n17; and Scripture, 126; self-criticism of, 196; social activism of, 12–14, 20, 78–79; social theories of, 16–17, 41, 44, 47, 55, 111; stroke suffered by, 14, 20, 31, 79, 140, 157, 182, 196; and Union Theological Seminary, 21, 23, 26, 32, 101–4, 110–11, 112; Wheat and the Tares sermon of, 36–39, 42, 54, 197; at Yale Divinity School, 3–4

Niebuhr, Reinhold, writings of: "Augustine and Political Realism," 225n20; *The Children of Light and the Children of Darkness,* 140–42; *Christian Realism and Political Problems,* 157; *The Democratic Experience,* 157; *An Interpretation of Christian Ethics,* 85–86, 110; *The Irony of American History,* 151, 154, 157, 179, 187–88, 190, 198; *Leaves from the Notebook of a Tamed Cynic,* 15, 20–21, 86; *Man's Nature and His Communities,* 14, 157; *Moral Man,* see *Moral Man and Immoral Society; The Nature and Destiny of Man,* 77, 108–13, 122–25, 126, 135–37, 139–41, 157, 159, 180; *Reflections on the End of an Era,* 126, 137; scholarship in, 110–11; *The Self and the Dramas of History,* 157; *The Structure of Nations and Empires,* 157, 182; "A View of Life from the Sidelines" (memoir), 196–97; *The World Crisis and American Responsibility,* 157

Niebuhr, Richard (brother), 6, 110
Niebuhr, Richard Reinhold (nephew), 6
Niebuhr, Ursula (wife), 6
Nixon, Richard M., 165, 177, 187

Obama, Barack, xi–xii
oligarchy, 82
"O Master, Let Me Walk With Thee" (Gladden), 18, 216n16
"Ought" vs. "Is," 85, 95
Oxford Group, 195

parables, irony in, 37–38, 42
Parks, Rosa, 94
pastors: calls on parishioners by, 15–16; children of, 5; as community leaders, 4–5; congregations' expectations of, 15–16, 64, 66, 67, 70, 71; homilies of, 107; human failings of, 71; inspiration sought from, 71; as itinerant preachers, 64; legitimate authority of, 67; moral perfection displayed by, 5; parsonages of, 5; and power, 82; preaching, 16, 63–68; preaching The Gospel, 32–35; prophetic, 147; pulpits of, 63–68; sermons of, 33–34, 36–39, 64–65; training of, 67
Paul, Saint, 33, 147, 204; on Christ as messiah, 128; and the inward man, 113, 126–28; Letter to the Romans, 105; as pastor, 105; and theory of history, 129
Pauline theology, 104–5, 126

Peace of Westphalia, 150, 153
perfectionism, 18, 159; Christianity's inclination toward, 61–62; and Marxism, 89–90; reconciliation with imperfection, 70
Persian Empire, 130
personality, discovery of, 127
philosophical ethics, 85
piety, 26, 186
Plato, 109, 127
political oppression, 48
power: amoral, xv–xvi; checks and balances against, 177–78; as coercion, 57–58, 59, 60, 88–89; and conservatives, 143; of corporations, 96; definition of, 176; distortions and lies of, 88–89, 199; and domination, 176; economic, 57, 73; of God, 185; of the human spirit, 42; imperial, 58; and innocence, 198, 202; and liberalism, 47–48, 52–53, 74, 143, 172; and the ministry, 82; in modern societies, 56–57; political, 57, 73, 82, 98, 172, 177; of the pulpit, 63–71, 86–87, 89; secular, 73; and social injustice, 56; socialism's doctrines of, 74; of the state, 47–48, 49, 52, 55–61, 78, 96, 152, 154; state corruption of, 60; subjugation to, 88–89, 90; suspicion of, 49, 81–82, 176–78; theory of, 57–58, 222–23n42; of the weak, 80
powerlessness, human value of, 195
preachers. See pastors

Press, Samuel D., 138, 145–47
pride, 69, 79, 143, 160, 185, 203
priest, sacred rites performed by, 67
progress, liberal ideals of, xiii,
122, 190
Progressive Era, 17
Protestantism: churches, appeal of,
82–84; cultural differences
within, 10, 189; and despair,
68–69; direct route to God in, 83;
doctrines within, 9; ecumenical,
10; evangelical, *see* evangelical
Protestantism; excitable religious
sentiment in, 69; faith of, 69–70,
71, 83–84; five solas of, 221n26;
fundamentalist, 67, 189; Great
Awakening, 184, 185; historic
importance of, 174; history
distorted by, 182; hypocrisy in,
62; and individualism, 173–76;
influence of, 65; mergers within,
10; and modern culture, 53, 65;
moral individualism in, 16,
82–83, 174–75; mystery in, 34, 68;
and national religion, 182–90;
populations of, 173–74; power of
the pulpit in, 63–71, 86–87;
preaching The Gospel, 32–35,
39–40; rebirth in, 67–68;
reconciliation with imperfection,
70; and Reformation, 34, 40, 126,
147; and sermons, 33–34, 36–39,
64–65; and Social Gospel, *see*
Social Gospel movement; truths
of, 68
Protestant principle, 83–84, 125,
176, 189

pulpits: as cultural institution, 65; as
dangerous, 70; human elements
in, 71; platform of, 87, 98;
political, 65; power of, 63–71,
86–87, 89; in Protestant
churches, 65–71
Puritanism, 9, 108, 109–10, 175

Qing dynasty, 168

rabbi, as teacher, 67
rabbits vs. turtles, 152
rationalism, 184, 186
Rauschenbusch, Walter, 17–18, 53
Reagan, Ronald, 206–7; "evil
empire" of, xii
realism, xiii, 85; Christian, 25,
43–44, 75, 136–37, 159; as
evolving biblical theology, 55,
77–78; liberal, 11; philosophical,
44; political, xv, 47, 77, 78, 145,
159, 160, 166, 216n17; postliberal
left, 76; for the powerful, 77,
81–82; religious, 44, 160
recovery, political, 208
recovery programs, 193–95
Red Scare, 167, 171
Reformation, 34, 40, 126, 147
Reformed Church, 8, 9, 174
religion: biblical, 55, 84; civil,
182–90; Great Awakening, 184,
185; and higher power, 35;
historical, 137–38; and human
frailty, 43; and liberalism, 47, 55;
love and benevolence encouraged
in, 61–62; messiah in, 138;
mystery of, 34, 68; organized, 180;

religion (continued)

 otherworldly, 82; perfectionism
 in, 61–62, 70; and piety, 26, 186;
 and recovery programs, 193–95;
 revivalism, 187; as social force, 18;
 tolerance of, 8, 9

religious right, 79, 187, 189

Renaissance, 109

Reuther, Walter, 79

Riesman, David, 178; *The Lonely
 Crowd,* 170

robber barons, 73

Roman Empire, 129–31, 133–34, 153

Romanticism, 186

Rome: the Church in, 34;
 corruption of, 134; decline of, 132,
 137; sack of, 130, 134

Roosevelt, Eleanor, 79

Roosevelt, Franklin D., 156, 202, 205;
 election of, 46, 75, 177; and liberal
 policies, 50, 143, 177; social
 programs of, 26–27, 50, 54, 78

Roosevelt, Theodore, 177

Rousseau, Jean-Jacques, 182

Royce, Josiah, 112

Russia: in Cold War, *see* Soviet
 Union; commercial interests
 in, 198

salvation, 175, 221n26

Saul of Tarsus, 33

Schlesinger, Arthur, Jr., 25, 79

Schweitzer, Albert, 112

Scripture, salvation by, 221n26

secular humanity, 122

self: historical, 166; moral, 166–67;
 nature of, 127–28

self-consciousness, 114–15, 116–17,
 118–20

self-deception, 60

selfishness, 41, 60, 62, 77, 107–8,
 116, 118, 141

self-knowledge, 42

September 11 attacks, 25, 134,
 190, 199

serenity, 209–10

Serenity Prayer, 193–97, 213–14n4

sex, and sin, 107–10, 113

Sifton, Elisabeth (daughter):
 about Alcoholics Anonymous,
 195; *Serenity Prayer,* 6,
 232–33n1

sin, 106–8; arrogance of, 41–42, 43,
 107, 108; and fate, 121; general
 theory of, 41; as human problem,
 118–19, 128, 209; paradox of, 105;
 selfishness of, 41, 107–8, 116, 118;
 and sex, 107–10, 113; as a social
 thing, 121; for the unwashed
 (unbaptized), 41; use of term, 42,
 139, 144

Smith, Adam, 176

social conflict, cycle of, 87

social differences, 209

social ethic: compromises of,
 143; in *Moral Man,* 63, 85, 87,
 90–92, 95, 99, 112, 148; realistic,
 24, 41

Social Gospel movement, 44, 73,
 143; and Columbia University,
 102; emergence of, 17–19; fading
 influence of, 75–76, 77, 94; and
 liberalism, 24, 53, 54; and *Moral
 Man,* 53, 54, 76, 89; Niebuhr's

move to political realism from, 216n17; and theory of individual rights, 54

socialism, xiii, 27, 54; in Europe, 177; in France, 50; and liberalism, 91; and power, 74

social justice: biblical principles of, 54; in democracies, *see* democracy; and injustice, 55, 56, 87; and Wheat and the Tares sermon, 54

Soviet Union: and Cold War, 158, 162–72, 179, 182, 202–3; collapse of, 164, 165; hegemony of, 166, 171, 182; and Iron Curtain, 170; system of, 157, 158, 165

Sputnik, 163

Stalin, Joseph, 53, 90, 158; and Cold War, 164–65, 168, 202–3, 205; at Yalta, 162, 205

state: central authority of, 152; coercion by, 47, 57, 58, 59–60, 87, 88–89; cohesion of, 152–53; corruption of power in, 60, 169; distortions and lies of, 88–89, 154, 155–56; empires vs. nations, 153; idea and possibility of, 153; immorality of, 59–60, 97, 163; vs. individuals, 151, 154–57, 185; international achievements of, 61; messianistic hope in, 180; as modern invention, 149; mutual consent in, 47; nation-state, general theory of, 58–60; political being developed in, 152; power of, 47–48, 49, 52, 55–61, 78, 96, 152, 154; revolutionary origins of,

152; sovereignty of, 153–54, 179; subjugation by, 88–89; use of force by, 59; welfare programs of, 49

Stendhal, Krister, 211

Stevenson, Adlai E., 156

stock market crash (1929), 12, 21, 73, 76, 103, 106, 112, 125, 202

Stoics, 109

subjugation, 88–89

subjugation theory of power, 90

Taylor, Frederick Winslow, 220n13

Thrasymachus, 176

Tillich, Paul, 83–84, 112

Tocqueville, Alexis de, *American Democracy,* 172–73, 180–81

Tories, as conservatives, 49

Trajan, Emperor, 129

transition, times of, xiv–xv

Truman, Harry S., 156, 167

truth, 156, 159

turtles vs. rabbits, 152

twelve-step programs, 193–95, 233–34n5

understanding, and self, 127–28

Union for Democratic Action (UDA), 78–79

Union Theological Seminary, New York: and Jewish Theological Seminary, 103, 150; Niebuhr's work in, 21, 23, 26, 32, 101–4, 110–11, 112

United Church of Christ (UCC), 11

United States: changes within, 76; as Christian nation, 174; and Cold War, 142, 158, 161, 162–72, 179, 181–82, 187–88, 190, 200–203; commercial interests of, 201; foundational values of, 80–81, 98; hegemony of, 139, 142, 151, 166, 171–72, 179, 181, 182, 198–200; individualism in, 171–74; and manifest destiny, 181; messianism of, 180, 182; military budgets of, 200–201; patriotism in, 180; productivity in, 164, 178; Red Scare in, 167, 171; as sole superpower, 172; in World War II, 164, 201

us vs. them: either/or, 49; Manichean principle of, 25–26

utopian ideals, 20, 125, 160

values, xv, 54–55, 80–81, 85, 98

Velvet Revolution, 158

Versailles Treaty (1919), 20

Vietnam Syndrome, 199

Vietnam War, 162–63, 168, 180

votes, competition for, 50

Wallerstein, Immanuel, 153

war, when reason fails, 153

Way, the, 36–39, 40

wealth gap, 82, 207

Weber, Max, 57, 155, 180; A vs. B powers, 52–53, 176; *Protestant Ethic and the Spirit of Capitalism,* 174–75

welfare state, 176

Wesley, John, 40

West, decline of, xiv

Westphalia, Peace of, 150, 153

What is to be done? 95, 191

What now? xiv–xv

Wheat and the Tares, sermon, 36–39, 42, 54, 197

Whigs, as Liberals, 48–49

White, Hayden, 131–32

White, William H., 170

Whitehead, Alfred North, *Process and Reality,* 111–12

will, and self, 127

Wolfe, Alan, *The Future of Liberalism,* 51

work, hard, 175

world, end of, 40

World War I, 16, 58, 202; effects of, 86, 103; and *Moral Man,* 112; and Versailles, 20

World War II, 27, 86, 106, 190; and *Children of Light,* 141; and Cold War, 158, 171; and fascism, 112, 113, 158; and Japan, 168; legacy of, 206; and Niebuhr's lecture tours, 112–13; and postwar recovery, 104, 151, 154; U.S. productivity in, 164, 201

Wright City, Missouri, 1–3

Xerxes, Emperor, 130

Yale Divinity School, 3–4

Yalta conference, 158, 162, 205

YMCA, 19

Charles Lemert is the John C. Andrus Professor of Social Theory Emeritus at Wesleyan University and Senior Fellow of the Center for Comparative Research in Sociology at Yale. He is the author most recently of *The Structural Lie: Small Clues to Global Things* (Paradigm, 2011) and *Globalization: A Reader* (ed. with Anthony Elliott, Daniel Chaffee, and Eric Hsu; Routledge, 2010). Lemert received his Ph.D. from Harvard University in 1972 after graduating from Andover Newton Theological School. In this book he returns to one of his early interests in social ethics and moral realism in American culture.